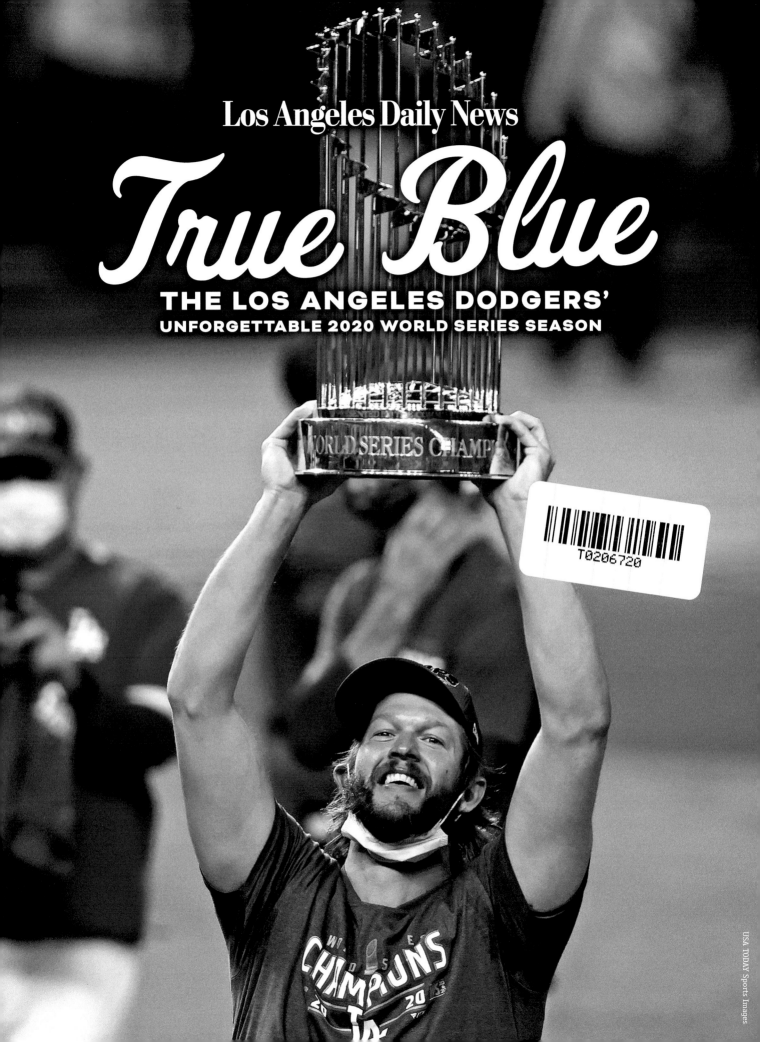

Los Angeles Daily News

True Blue

THE LOS ANGELES DODGERS'
UNFORGETTABLE 2020 WORLD SERIES SEASON

WORLD SERIES CHAMPIONS

T0206720

USA TODAY Sports Images

Copyright © 2020 Southern California News Group

No part of this publication may be reproduced, stored in a retrieval system or transmitted in any form by
any means, electronic, mechanical, photocopying or otherwise, without prior written permission of the publisher,
Triumph Books LLC, 814 North Franklin Street; Chicago, Illinois 60610.

This book is available in quantity at special discounts for your group or organization.
For further information, contact:

Triumph Books LLC
814 North Franklin Street
Chicago, Illinois 60610
Phone: (312) 337-0747
www.triumphbooks.com

Printed in U.S.A.
ISBN: 978-1-62937-816-9

Southern California News Group
Ron Hasse, President & Publisher
Bill Van Laningham, Vice President, Marketing
Frank Pine, Executive Editor
Tom Moore, Executive Sports Editor
Michele Cardon and Dean Musgrove, Photo Editors

Content packaged by Mojo Media, Inc.
Joe Funk: Editor
Jason Hinman: Creative Director

This is an unofficial publication. This book is in no way affiliated with, licensed by or endorsed
by Major League Baseball, the Los Angeles Dodgers or any associated entities.

AP Images

Contents

Introduction

By Bill Plunkett • October 27, 2020

Thirty-two years is a long time.

Long enough for Dodgers fans to wonder if this day might never come. And it nearly didn't. From Oct. 20, 1988 when Orel Hershiser threw the last pitch of the Dodgers' five-game World Series victory over the Oakland A's until Tuesday night, when Julio Urias did the same against the Tampa Bay Rays – a franchise that didn't even exist in 1988 – the Dodgers and their fans went into the winter year after year feeling disappointed – or cheated.

But 2020 was different – in so many, many ways.

"This year is our year," Dodgers manager Dave Roberts said to the mostly-empty stands at Globe Life Field after accepting the National League Championship Trophy a week and a half ago.

"This is our year."

He was right. The Dodgers made it theirs Tuesday night with a 3-1 victory in Game 6, the best team in baseball at every step of the challenges 2020 presented.

"This is our year," Roberts repeated upon accepting the World Series trophy, the 11,000 or so fans in attendance giving voice to so many more. "We said it."

But how many times had "this is our year" been said over the previous 32 years – bragging or begging, in the pavilions at Dodger Stadium or family barbecues around the Southland?

Thirty-two years is a long time.

Long enough for 18 different franchises to celebrate a fresh championship while the Dodgers' '88 win grew stale. Two franchises that didn't even exist in 1988 (the Florida/Miami Marlins and Arizona Diamondbacks) won

championships. Two curses ended (the Boston Red Sox in 2004, the Chicago Cubs in 2016, both after stepping over the Dodgers in the playoffs). Even worse for Dodger fans, the San Francisco Giants – their hated rivals – celebrated three championships in a five-year span. Even the Angels, the little brother and former tenant, won a title under the leadership of a once-favored Dodger son, Mike Scioscia.

Thirty-two years is a long time.

Long enough for the franchise to change hands three times, going from O'Malley family ownership to Fox corporate ownership into the hands of a parking lot owner with strange ideas about other people's money and finally to the Guggenheim Group, which seems to have all the money.

The franchise had grown stale in the '90s as baseball's economic realities made family ownership increasingly difficult. The corporate overlords from Fox didn't stick around for long – but long enough to alienate a generation of fans when they ended a financial standoff with slugging catcher Mike Piazza by trading the future Hall of Famer for a pocketful of beans that had no magic in them.

Then along came Frank McCourt and an eight-year soap opera. Houses were collected for their swimming pools. A future football exec (Paul DePodesta) was hired and fired less than two years later. A Russian physicist named Vladimir Shpunt with healing powers that worked through your TV was paid hundreds of thousands of dollars to infuse "V energy" into the team.

It all ended in bankruptcy, divorce (the costliest in California history by at least one reckoning) and fan

Corey Seager was named the MVP of the World Series after hitting .400, with two home runs, five RBIs and six walks. (AP Images)

boycotts. But the McCourts came out smelling fine after selling the team to the Guggenheim Group for a then-record $2.1 billion. Frank owns the L.A. Marathon and a French soccer team now. Jamie badly miscalculated her share of the Dodger sale but is the U.S. Ambassador to France and Monaco now. One son, Drew, is part of the plan to put a gondola downtown to transport fans to Dodger Stadium.

Thirty-two years is a long time.

Long enough for so many players to come and go. From Ashley (Billy) to Zeile (Todd), E.D. (Eric Davis) to E.K. (Eric Karros), Grudzielanek (Mark) to Mientkiewicz (Doug) to Federowicz (Tim), Howell (Jay) to Howell (J.P.), Brown (Kevin) to Green (Shawn) to White (Devon), Candelaria (John) to Candiotti (Tom), Ely (John) to Lilly (Ted), Clark (Dave) to Kent (Jeff), Mulholland (Terry) to Ventura (Robin).

Hall of Famers started their careers in Dodger blue (Piazza and Pedro Martinez) or stopped by on their final laps before Cooperstown (Eddie Murray, Rickey Henderson, Gary Carter and Greg Maddux).

Since Orel Hershiser struck out Oakland's Tony Phillips for the final out of the 1988 Series, the Dodgers have played 5,014 regular-season games and 113 more in the postseason in pursuit of their next title. They have spent $3.69 billion in player payroll over 32 seasons.

Thirty-two years is a long time.

Long enough for the familiar fist-pumping highlight of Kirk Gibson homering off Dennis Eckersley to become a bit of an irritant to the current Dodgers.

"I got drafted by the Dodgers. I didn't know a ton of Dodger history at the time," pitcher Clayton Kershaw said on the eve of the 2017 World Series. "But coming up, it kind of gets ingrained in you, which is a good thing. It's not a lot of organizations that have the type of history that the Dodgers do.

"It's been a special thing, and I hope after this week is over, they can talk about 2017 a little more and 1988 a lot less."

Kershaw got half of his wish. People do talk an awful lot about 2017. An awful lot.

Thirty-two years is a long time.

Long enough to get used to new voices and say goodbye to old ones.

It might have been the most perfectly brilliant moment in a career filled with them.

"High fly ball into right field, she is gone! … In a year

that has been so improbable, the impossible has happened."

Vin Scully was 60 years old that night, completing his 39th season as the Dodgers' play-by-play announcer. Revered. Iconic. He grew in stature but retired after 67 seasons in 2016 never having called games for another Dodger World Series team.

Thirty-two years is a long time.

Long enough for us all to endure the longest year of our lives.

Confidence that the long wait for a World Series title might finally end was at a 32-year high this spring. The Dodgers took a big swing and connected, trading for Mookie Betts on the eve of spring training. He would be the 21st century Gibson, they hoped, the difference-maker who would take them over the top.

But spring training came to an abrupt halt on a rainy night in Arizona in mid-March. The coronavirus pandemic had invaded the sports world as it would eventually envelop everything. Players were sent home, told to stay healthy, stay ready – but stay away.

"Yeah, it was weird. There were some days that you would go work out and you're like, man, I don't even know if we're gonna have a season this year," outfielder Cody Bellinger said. "And then you read up on social media and, oh okay. Things are looking good. We're gonna have a season and then just kind of go back and forth, back and forth."

The sport shut down for four months. How could anyone think of a World Series to crown a champion when Opening Day was an unknown?

"I was throwing sim games in May and June in Dallas, thinking about, man, are we even going to play a season?" Kershaw said. "Is this going to be a wasted year in everybody's career and things like that? Is it gonna be a wasted year for the Dodgers with the team that we have?"

MLB returned in July with health and safety protocols, constant testing, empty stadiums and fake crowd noise. There were outbreaks around the league but the Dodgers forged on, staying healthy and focused while winning game after game in front of cardboard cutouts instead of fans.

Thirty-two years is a long time.

Long enough for Southern California's two favorite franchises to get back in sync.

In 1988, the Lakers and Dodgers were both champions. They are again … after both living in a bubble to do it … and beating Florida-based franchises in their final series just weeks apart.

Thirty-two years is a long time.

Long enough to get rich … and smart. With the hiring of Andrew Friedman following the 2014 season, the Dodgers signaled their desire to pair their financial muscle with a new-age approach to statistical analysis, roster management, in-game strategy and player development.

Friedman, the president of baseball operations, inherited a talented roster, one that had already started a string of eight (and counting) consecutive division titles and been to the NLCS in 2013.

But he made it better. Investment in the farm system produced a steady stream of talent at the major-league level and fodder for mid-season gap-filling trades.

The division titles continued. NL pennants followed in 2017 and 2018, the first since 1988. Betts was acquired – and signed to a 12-year, $365 million contract extension at a time when there was reason to wonder if he'd ever play one game in a Dodger uniform.

The long-awaited championship was closer than it had been in decades.

"It's just a great team," Kershaw said. "I think top to bottom Andrew did a great job. He put together a great group of guys. We've got, I think, a great clubhouse. Everybody seems to get along pretty well. A lot of guys who can make people laugh, which I think is important. You've got a lot of guys who are down to business, which is important. And you got a ton of talent, which is really important."

Thirty-four days is a long time, too.

That's how long the Dodgers spent quarantined, the last 24 in their Texas "bubble", their world limited to a local resort hotel and the Texas Rangers' brand-new ballpark, Globe Life Field.

"Bubble life is – it's interesting," catcher Austin Barnes said.

Unlike the regular season, when players on the road were encouraged to stay in their rooms as much as possible and not mingle with the general public, playoff teams have stayed in a hotel devoted to them (the Dodgers shared that hotel with the San Diego Padres then the Atlanta Braves then the Rays as the postseason progressed).

With no public allowed in, the players could mingle in outdoor spaces. There was a game room for the players and their families – skee ball, ping pong and more at the ready. And there was a Halloween set-up for the "kiddos" – Kershaw's label for the toddler set.

Family members in the bubble could attend the games at Globe Life Field, seated in private areas down each foul line. Families not in the bubble had to content themselves with being among the limited number of fans in the stands, distanced from the players.

It was a strange arrangement for Dodgers like Kershaw, Max Muncy and Dustin May, who grew up and/ or live in the Dallas area with homes just minutes away from the hotel and ballpark that defined the parameters of their life for a month.

"It's been extremely difficult," Muncy said during Week Three of life in a bubble.

"You're so close, yet you're so far away. This has been home for me for the past 19, 20 years almost. It's home to me and my wife. It's where we have our house. Not being able to go and see that, see our friends, see our family – not even allowed to have our pets – it's just been extremely difficult.

"But we're really close to the end and hopefully it's all going to be worth it."

The end, of course, included a twist. Third baseman Justin Turner, one of the longest-tenured Dodgers, tested positive for COVID-19 and was pulled from the game in the seventh inning, unable to storm the field with his teammates afterward. MLB commissioner Rob Manfred confirmed the positive test after the game, telling Fox: "It's a bittersweet night for us."

Thirty-two years is a long time.

Long enough to become the best team in baseball.

They found out in the National League Championship Series against the Braves, losing the first two games and falling behind 3-1 in the best-of-seven series before rallying to reach the World Series for a third time in four years.

A relentless offense set a postseason record for two-out runs and Roberts pulled all the right strings – well, enough of them – to beat the Rays in six games.

"We're bringing the trophy home," Friedman said following Game 6. "Sorry it took so long. Thank you for your patience. But this trophy is coming home where it belongs."

Thirty-two years is such a long time. ∎

October 20, 2020 • Arlington, Texas
Dodgers 8, Rays 3

Opening Statement

Dodgers Take World Series Opener as Offense Stings Rays

By Bill Plunkett

Celebrate responsibly.

His right shoulder still sore from the overamped forearm bash that popped it out on Sunday, Cody Bellinger ditched the forearm but kept the bash, opting for foot taps all around after clubbing a two-run home run in the fourth inning of World Series Game 1 on Tuesday night.

"I said it today before the game," Bellinger said. "I said, 'If I hit one today, I'm not touching anybody's arm. I'm going straight foot.' It was pretty funny."

That was just the beginning of the celebratory moments for the Dodgers, who gave Clayton Kershaw the kind of support he has always deserved in the postseason and went on to beat the Tampa Bay Rays, 8-3, at Globe Life Field.

The winner of Game 1 has gone on to win the World Series 72 times including 21 of the past 26 years (though not in 2017).

"If we play at our best — no," Kershaw said with surprising candor after the game when he was asked if anyone could beat the Dodgers when they are playing well. "I think we are the best team and I think our clubhouse believes that. There's going to be certain times when we get beat. That happens. But as a collective group, if everybody is doing what they're supposed to be doing and playing the way they're supposed to, I don't see how that can happen."

That sounded like visions of a championship party are dancing in Kershaw's head after such a decisive win in the opener against the Rays.

"It's hard not to think about winning. It's hard not to think about what that might feel like," he admitted. "But I think that's what I have to do. I think that's what we have to do as a team is — just tomorrow. Just constantly keep putting that in your brain. Win tomorrow. Win tomorrow. Win tomorrow. And then you do that three more times and you can think about it all you want. It is hard not to let that creep in."

Before the Dodgers could, it was Rays starter Tyler Glasnow who announced his presence with authority in the first inning. Six of his 19 pitches were 99 mph — or faster. Through three innings, the Dodgers had just one hit, had drawn two walks and struck out five times.

But Max Muncy led off the fourth inning by drawing a walk — his 16th in 14 games this postseason.

Two batters later, Bellinger turned on a 98-mph first-pitch fastball and drove it into the right field seats. Bellinger clearly enjoys the heat — it was his fourth career at-bat against the hard-throwing Glasnow and third home run (the first two coming in 2018 when Glasnow was still with the Pittsburgh Pirates).

"I don't know. I really don't," Bellinger said, unable to explain that success rate. "He's got really good stuff. Today was just a moment where I tried to get the run in and stayed simple with it."

Glasnow walked Chris Taylor and struck out two to finish off the inning but he threw 30 pitches in the process, pushing his pitch count for the game to 86. Known for their foresight and missionary adherence to the gospel of numbers, the Rays nonetheless sent Glasnow back out to

Cody Bellinger circles the bases after hitting a two-run home run in the fourth inning. (AP Images)

face the Dodgers' lineup a third time starting with the fifth inning.

Mookie Betts and Corey Seager greeted him by drawing two more walks. Justin Turner struck out but Betts and Seager pulled off a double steal (as they had to great effect in Game 2 of the NLDS against the Padres).

Betts wasn't done. When Muncy bounced a ball to first baseman Yandy Diaz, Betts had taken such an aggressive secondary lead that he beat Diaz's throw home with a headfirst dive even though the Rays had been playing the infield in.

"Stolen bases are a thing for me," Betts said. "That's how I create runs, cause a little havoc on the bases. I take pride in stealing bases. Once I get on the bases, I'm just trying to touch home and however I get there is how I get there. I'm going to be aggressive on the basepaths."

With his dive, Betts became the first player to walk and steal multiple bases in an inning during the World Series since Babe Ruth did it in Game 2 of the 1921 World Series.

Wonder if those two guys have anything else in common.

Rays manager Kevin Cash stayed with Glasnow for one more batter and Will Smith singled in another run on Glasnow's 112th pitch — the most any Rays pitcher has thrown in a game this season. That they came in just 4-1/3 innings made it the shortest start by a pitcher who threw at least 110 pitches in a postseason game since postseason pitch counts were first tracked in 1988.

The Dodgers greeted his replacement, lefty Ryan Yarbrough, with back-to-back two-out RBI singles by Taylor and Kiké Hernandez, making it a four-run inning against a team whose only true superpower is run prevention.

Betts took a different route to creating a run in the sixth, leading off with a home run, making him the second player to homer and steal two bases in a World Series game (Chase Utley did it for the Phillies in 2008, also in a Game 1 against the Rays) and the first to do it while scoring twice.

"Mookie's pretty special," Kershaw said. "He does things on a baseball field that not many people can do. And he does it very consistently which I think separates him from a lot of guys."

Back-to-back doubles by Turner and Muncy made it 8-1 and Kershaw had one of the easiest nights of his tortured postseason life. It took him a moment to find his slider (he missed the strike zone with it six of eight times in the first inning) but Kershaw eventually carved up the Rays' weak lineup with it. The Rays swung 38 times at Kershaw's pitches and missed 19 times. He allowed a solo home run to Kevin Kiermaier in the fifth but just one other hit while striking out eight to become second all-time in postseason strikeouts (201, four behind Justin Verlander).

"We talked after that (first) inning and he said he'd find it and he did," Dodgers catcher Austin Barnes said. "We got a lot of swings and misses with it, made a lot of big pitches with it. It was that prototypical Kershaw slider that was working."

Upholding an October tradition, the Dodgers' bullpen allowed two runs in Kershaw's wake but lefty reliever Victor Gonzalez snared a 105.6 mph liner back at him, turning it into a double play to end the seventh and Bellinger made another great catch at the wall in the ninth inning to shut things down. ■

Known for his clever and aggressive baserunning, Mookie Betts scores on a fielder's choice by Max Muncy in the fifth inning. (AP Images)

World Series Game 2

October 21, 2020 • Arlington, Texas
Rays 6, Dodgers 4

Not as Planned

Dodgers' Pitching Strategy Puts Them in a Hole, Rays Take Game 2 to Even Series

By Bill Plunkett

A lot of things sound good in planning meetings. There was probably a lot of talk of synergy and collaboration as the Dodgers exhausted bandwidth and searched for a scalable paradigm that would allow them to Johnny Wholestaff their way through Game 2. There would be a cat-loving iteration of Johnny (Tony Gonsolin), a red-headed iteration of Johnny (Dustin May), a left-handed iteration of Johnny (Victor Gonzalez), a sassy iteration of Johnny (Joe Kelly) and so on. The different iterations would confound the Tampa Bay Rays' hitters and the outs would add up to 27.

Yeah — it didn't work.

The Rays' offense came to life with Brandon Lowe hitting two home runs and they hung on to even the World Series with a 6-4 victory on Wednesday night at Globe Life Field.

Held without a hit until the fifth inning, the Dodgers slowly crawled back from a five-run hole and had the tying run at the plate in the eighth inning but couldn't finish the comeback.

The Series takes a day off Thursday before resuming with Game 3 on Friday night.

"We feel great," Dodgers manager Dave Roberts insisted when asked about the state of the team's starting pitching now. "We've got Walker going (in Game 3). We've got Julio going (in Game 4) then we've got Clayton (in Game 5). You look at where our relievers are set with the off-day tomorrow — we're in a great spot."

They were stuck between a rock and a hard spot in Game 2, though, with no rested starter ready to go two days after the seven-games-in-seven-days NLCS ended.

"I think the biggest impact has been on our pitchers," Dodgers utility man Chris Taylor said. "Only one day off from a hard-fought seven-game series against the Braves. I think that showed a little bit today. We didn't have all of our guys available and some of the guys were throwing on short rest or no rest. A day off would definitely be nice, especially for our arms."

The Dodgers' relay team was facing a Rays lineup that hasn't hit much this postseason (a .208 team batting average through Game 1). But they have hit home runs, a postseason record-setting 28 of them after Lowe broke out of a 6-for-56 slump (.107) in the playoffs.

Gonsolin fell behind 3-and-1 to Lowe, the second batter in the game, before giving up a solo home run in the first inning. Lowe added a two-run home run off Dustin May in the fifth.

"I hit the first one and it was like a weight came off my shoulders," said Lowe, who led the Rays with 14 home runs during the regular season but had just one extra-base hit in the postseason before Game 2. "I was happy to finally be contributing to a team that has carried me through this so far."

Gonsolin and May could be forgiven if they feel they are being asked to carry the weight of the world. They have said all the right things about the way they have been deployed this postseason, not complaining or making excuses. But both pitched Sunday in Game 7 of the NLCS and only had two days off before taking the mound again Wednesday. The Dodgers got 5-2/3 innings out of them in these two "bullpen" games — but they allowed a combined seven runs.

"It's a big ask, to be quite frank," Roberts admitted after some post-game prodding. "Right now, with the off days, every team is going to go down a starter so that's one thing. So people have to adjust to certain roles. And when you're talking about playing seven days in a row and how you can get as many outs as you can in the LCS — yeah, these guys are in uncharted territory.

"Credit to them — they're not making excuses. They expect themselves to make pitches. It's different certainly. But we still need those guys to get important outs going

Corey Seager's eighth-inning home run kept the Dodgers' threat of a comeback alive, if only momentarily. (AP Images)

forward if we're going to win this thing."

Joey Wendle doubled in two runs with two outs in the fourth after Kiké Hernandez and Corey Seager weren't quick enough to turn a potential inning-ending double play on Ji-Man Choi. That was also off May, who has been more eager than effective in the hybrid role the Dodgers have assigned him this postseason. In four appearances in the NLCS against the Braves and now in the World Series, May has allowed six runs in his past six innings.

But he wasn't alone. The Rays scored runs off four of the Dodgers' first five pitchers and were up 5-0 before the Dodgers got their first hit. In the first six innings, only Dylan Floro emerged unscathed and that was courtesy of the Dodgers' defense. With the infield in and runners at the corners, Seager cut off one run at the plate and Will Smith made a perfect throw to catch Willy Adames on a steal attempt (thanks to a replay review).

Rays starter Blake Snell baffled the Dodgers with a slider that produced most of his nine strikeouts in the first 4-2/3 innings. The Dodgers worked him for two walks in the second inning but didn't have another baserunner until Hernandez drew a two-out walk in the bottom of the fifth.

Walks have been very good for the Dodgers this postseason and Hernandez's extended the inning long enough for No. 9 hitter Chris Taylor to push a hanging curveball on the outside part of the plate over the wall in right field. The opposite-field, two-run home run was the Dodgers' first hit of the game and breathed life into their lineup.

An inning later, Smith drove another curveball — this one from Rays reliever Nick Anderson — over the wall in left field. And in the eighth, Seager led off with his seventh home run of this postseason, sending a slider from Pete Fairbanks over the wall in center field. All seven of Seager's postseason home runs have been hit in the games at Globe Life Field — more than any Texas Ranger hit in their 30 home games during the regular season — and are the most by any shortstop in a single postseason.

When Justin Turner followed Seager's latest homer with a double, the Dodgers had the tying run at the plate. But Muncy flied out and Smith hit a 102.6 mph bullet right to Wendle at third base. Cody Bellinger took a called third strike to end the threat.

That was as close as they could get, finishing 0 for 6 with runners in scoring position. But the Dodgers took heart in having gotten a first-hand look at the Rays' best relievers — Anderson, Fairbanks and Diego Castillo — in a game that could have been a runaway.

"It's great, just to put eyes on guys we hadn't seen before," Roberts said. "Once you see guys once, twice you just keep getting that familiarity and that's only going to benefit us going forward. That's a credit to our offense, just continuing to fight and claw to make sure those leverage guys got in the game tonight." ∎

October 23, 2020 • Arlington, Texas
Dodgers 6, Rays 2

Keeping Up the Pressure

Dodgers Torment Rays with Two-Out Hits, Take World Series Game 3

By Bill Plunkett

Just when you think you're out — they pull you back in.

The Dodgers' offense has been ruthless this postseason when opposing pitchers start to peek toward the dugout, wondering which flavor Gatorade (the ubiquitous beverage of the postseason) they will swig with satisfaction after retiring the side.

Five times on Friday night the Tampa Bay Rays pitchers were one out away from sweet hydration when the Dodgers scored. The two-out torment carried the Dodgers to a 6-2 victory over the Rays in World Series Game 3.

The win gives the Dodgers a 2-1 lead in the best-of-seven series.

"Just not giving up. Obviously, there's two outs but you can still build an inning," Dodgers outfielder Mookie Betts said. "Not giving away at-bats. I think that's the recipe for that. And that's how you win a World Series, so we have to continue to do that for two more games."

Fifty of the Dodgers' 87 runs this postseason have scored after there were two outs in an inning. It is the most by any team in the wild-card era (since 1999). Take away the four two-out runs they scored in the extra round Wild Card Series against the Milwaukee Brewers and they still would be tied with the 2004 Boston Red Sox for the wild-card era high.

"Being that I've been on the other side, it's tough," Betts said of the way a two-out rally can demoralize opposing pitchers. "You're one out away. Then a walk here, a single here, a double here. The next thing you know you've given up a couple runs. It's kind of tough to stop the bleeding. I think we've done a good job keeping up the pressure."

Rays starter Charlie Morton came into Game 3 with 10-2/3 scoreless innings in the American League Championship Series under his belt. That streak didn't make it out of the first inning. Justin Turner drove a 1-and-2 fastball from Morton into the left field seats — with two outs.

The home run was the 11th of Turner's postseason career, tying Duke Snider for the franchise record.

Two innings later, Turner's two-out double set up a two-run single by Max Muncy. It was Turner's 18th postseason double, tying him with Chipper Jones and Albert Pujols for the second most in National League history (behind Yadier Molina's 19).

"Something that's pretty cool, that I can talk about when I'm done playing," Turner said of his standing on the postseason leaderboards. "But it doesn't mean a whole lot until we finish this thing off and we win two more games."

Turner's glove played a crucial role as well. In the bottom of the third, he snared a hard-hit ground ball by Mike Zunino and turned it into an inning-ending double play that kept Walker Buehler's no-hitter going a little longer.

Morton failed to live up to his reputation as a clutch

Austin Barnes lays down an RBI bunt in the fourth inning of the Game 3 win. Barnes would later follow up with a solo home run, his first of the postseason. (AP Images)

THE LOS ANGELES DODGERS' UNFORGETTABLE 2020 WORLD SERIES SEASON

performer in the postseason — he was 7-0 in his previous nine appearances with the Rays and Houston Astros, dating to 2017. But Buehler just added another layer to his big-game armor.

Buehler overpowered the Rays' lineup, retiring 12 of the first 13 batters he faced, six on strikeouts. The lone blip was a walk to Kevin Kiermaier, erased moments later by Turner's play.

A pair of doubles ended Buehler's no-hit run in the fifth inning and produced the Rays' only run off Buehler, who struck out 10 in six innings. It was the first time in World Series history a pitcher had packed a double-digit strikeout total into a six-inning start.

"He was unbelievable. … That might have been the best I've ever seen his stuff," Dodgers catcher Austin Barnes said.

"He had the ability to throw that curveball, keep them a little off balance and not on the heater when he had to. But I thought his fastball was special."

The two-out runs kept coming for the Dodgers in the fourth inning, this time after Barnes drove in a run with a safety squeeze bunt — the first sacrifice bunt by an NL team this postseason. (Welcome to the era of the universal designated hitter.)

"You get a situation like that and Morton is really tough on right-handed hitters. We've got a plus-runner at third base in Cody (Bellinger). I trust Austin handling the bat," Dodgers manager Dave Roberts said of the strategic decision. "Nothing against (Ji-Man) Choi at first base, I just don't think he's fleet of foot. So I felt if we could get something down on the right side of the infield we'd have a good chance of getting an insurance run and Austin did a good job of executing."

Betts followed Barnes to the plate with two outs and Joc Pederson on second. Betts fell behind 0-and-2, worked the count full, then slashed an RBI single to center field.

It was the 15th time this postseason a Dodger had come through with runners in scoring position after getting two strikes on him. The Dodgers have driven in 36 runs this postseason with two strikes on the batter, also a postseason record for the wild-card era.

Those situations have been kryptonite for the Dodgers in past postseasons. During their season-ending postseason series each of the past four years — the NLCS in 2016, the World Series in 2017 and 2018 and the NLDS in 2019 — the Dodgers batted .203 with runners in scoring position.

This year, they have gone 34 for 106 (.321) with RISP in the postseason — a major reason they are now just two wins away from their first World Series title since 1988.

"Just a credit to guys digging in and fighting and battling, not trying to do too much, just trying to move the ball forward and put something in play so good things can happen," Turner said.

"I think for the most part guys are just in there trying to get good pitches and hit the ball as hard as they can. Sometimes they go over the fence. Obviously not as many go over the fence here because it's a big yard. We've done a good job of finding barrels and hitting the ball hard. When you do that, you're going to get hits."

Barnes scored the Dodgers' final two-out run of the night in the sixth inning when he added a solo home run to his RBI sacrifice bunt, becoming only the third player in World Series history with that unique small ball-long ball combo.

And Barnes became the 11th Dodger to hit a home run this postseason.

None of those positive statistics are enough to make Turner look forward or feel that the Dodgers have taken command of the series.

"Absolutely not," he said. "We know how difficult this is. We know there's still a lot of work to do in front of us. Personally, we were down 3-1 in the last series and fought and clawed our way back. So you don't take anything for granted." ■

Walker Buehler was terrific in Game 3, striking out 10 in six innings and picking up the win. (AP Images)

October 24, 2020 • Arlington, Texas
Rays 8, Dodgers 7

Shell-Shocked

Dodgers Blow Lead After Lead, Lose Roller-Coaster Ride in Game 4
By Bill Plunkett

Six Flags Over Texas is located just down the road from Globe Life Field. It sits mostly empty these days, its rides still with the park all but shut down by the coronavirus pandemic.

It could have been going full bore. The Dodgers and Tampa Bay Rays still would have provided the best thrill ride in town Saturday night. And like the most extreme rides, some enjoyed it more than others.

"Man, baseball is fun. Wow," a breathless Brett Phillips said in a post-game interview just moments after his flare single set off a chain reaction of events — none of them good for the Dodgers — that led to the Rays walking off with an 8-7 victory in Game 4 that evened the best-of-seven World Series at two games apiece.

The Dodgers were one strike away from taking a 3-1 lead in the series with Clayton Kershaw scheduled to start Game 5. The baseball fates that have toyed with the Dodgers for 32 years — and future Hall of Famer Kershaw for the past eight — seemed to finally be aligning in their favor.

And then Lucy yanked the football away again.

"Wild game. Back and forth. Up and down," Dodgers third baseman Justin Turner said, his face flushed red during his post-game interview — a lingering reminder of the shell-shocked looks the Dodgers carried off the field.

"But like we've said all along, we know it's not going to be easy. We know how difficult this is. … Couple bobbles. Will (Smith) trying to turn around and put a quick tag on him, doesn't squeeze the ball and it trickles away. That was the ballgame."

Watching the deciding play was like watching a multi-car crash in slow motion. So many mistakes by so many people.

Kenley Jansen came in to protect a one-run lead in the ninth, but he gave up a broken-bat single to Kevin Kiermaier and walked Randy Arozarena to put the tying and go-ahead runs on base with two outs. Jansen got ahead 1-and-2, but Phillips dropped a flare into center field for his first hit since Sept. 25.

Chris Taylor started the game in left field and moved to center field mid-game with Cody Bellinger at DH due to back tightness. Taylor charged the ball and scooped it as he was looking up to see if Arozarena would go to third base.

He never secured the ball and his scoop just served to fling it away to his left, allowing Arozarena time to round third base and head home.

But Arozarena stumbled and fell and was about to turn back to third when he saw Max Muncy's relay throw home to Smith. Muncy's throw was to Smith's right and he reached for it then spun around looking to put a tag on Arozarena. The ball came loose in the process.

Jansen was standing on the infield grass between third and home, not backing up … anything. So Arozarena got up, finished his trip and practically belly-flopped on home plate to score the winning run while Smith scrambled to retrieve the ball.

"Honestly it's hard to believe right now that just happened," Phillips said. "Once I saw Randy slip, I thought, 'Oh, shoot at least we tied it up.'

"Then I don't know what happened, but he scored and the next thing I know I'm airplane-ing around and I get dogpiled."

The Rays — the home team 1,100 miles from their actual home — celebrated the first walk-off win in a World Series game since the Dodgers won Game 3 in 2018 on an

Cody Bellinger was hitless in four at bats as the Dodgers failed to hold on to Game 4 and take control of the series. (AP Images)

18th-inning home run by Muncy. It was the first walk-off win by a team that entered the final inning trailing since Joe Carter's home run decided the 1993 Series.

The Dodgers' conclusive bungling was the final flourish on a game that saw the two teams combine to score 12 runs in the fifth through ninth innings, scoring in eight consecutive half innings (the longest such streak in World Series history) from the bottom of the fourth through the top of the eighth and swapping the lead like a Netflix password.

Every pitching choice Dave Roberts made in Game 4 turned out as wrong as social media always thinks they do.

He pulled starter Julio Urias in the fifth inning in favor of Blake Treinen. Treinen got out of the inning but created trouble in the sixth and Roberts brought in Pedro Baez to face Brandon Lowe.

It was a decision based in some logic — left-handed hitters were 3 for 31 against Baez this season with no extra-base hits.

The next two left-handed hitters he faced hit home runs. Lowe upended a Dodger lead with a three-run home run. But Joc Pederson's two-out single in the top of

the seventh put the Dodgers back on top — and Roberts sent Baez back out for the bottom of the seventh. Two batters in, he gave up a game-tying home run to another left-handed hitter, Kevin Kiermaier.

"Lowe, I just loved the matchup," Roberts said. "I just felt Petey could pick Blake up right there. He had him 1-and-2, didn't execute a pitch and Lowe put a really good swing on it.

"That next inning, I take blame for having him go back out. We were down and I told him he was finished. So to ask him to go back out (after the Dodgers regained the lead) … He said he felt good. I shouldn't have said that and kept him burning a little bit."

Relievers on both sides kept trying to put out fires the rest of the night. Jansen was the last one to get burned.

"I didn't give up one hard hit. What can I do?" Jansen said accurately. The ninth-inning singles by Kiermaier and Phillips had exit velocities of 63.5 and 82.8 mph. "I threw the pitches where I wanted to. Credit to the hitters. A broken-bat single then a bloop single.

"Ain't no time to hang our heads. Tomorrow is another day." ∎

October 25, 2020 • Arlington, Texas
Dodgers 4, Rays 2

In Their Grasp

Dodgers Tilt World Series Back in Their Favor, Move Within One Win of Title

By Bill Plunkett

Can you taste it? Vindication with undertones of elation and relief, mixed with a lingering note of devastation.

It's that close.

The roof was closed to keep out the demons on Sunday night and the baseball fates that have toyed with the Dodgers for 32 years — and Clayton Kershaw for the past eight — took the night off, no doubt exhausted by their shenanigans a night earlier.

Kershaw recorded 15 outs, the Tampa Bay Rays chipped in two more with their baserunning and they didn't ask any more of their star-crossed future Hall of Famer, turning to the bullpen to hold fast to win Game 5, 4-2, and move within one game of their first World Series title since the year of Kershaw's birth.

It is the second time since 1988 — always, everything, since 1988 — the Dodgers have been this close. They were one win away in 2017, too. But the trash cans at Globe Life Field all seem to be accounted for and Yu Darvish will not be admitted for the final act in this drama.

Instead, it will be rookie right-hander Tony Gonsolin who gets the start with the Dodgers on the precipice of a championship. Pitching on just two days' rest, Gonsolin lasted only 1-1/3 innings in Game 2 against the Rays. He will be on five days' rest in Game 6 after a day off Monday for both sides to collect their thoughts.

The Dodgers will only have one.

"The off day is going to be hard tomorrow, I think," Kershaw said. "It's going to be good for us, resetting our bullpen and things like that, which is huge. But sitting around one win away from a World Series is going to be hard — especially when you've been in the same hotel for four weeks now.

"But I think we can wait one more day."

The Dodgers were so traumatized by their self-immolation in the ninth inning of Game 4 that it took them two whole batters to start scoring runs again in Game 5.

Mookie Betts led off with a ringing double into the left field corner and Corey Seager followed with an RBI single (part of a stretch of six consecutive plate appearances that ended with him reaching base). Ten pitches into the game the Dodgers had a lead. Joc Pederson and Max Muncy added to it with home runs.

But the focus became protecting that lead like a Faberge egg for the rest of the night.

Going into Game 5, the Dodgers had determined an outer limit for Kershaw — something they had been far too fickle about in past Octobers, leading to many of the scars Kershaw wears after being asked for too much on a postseason mound.

"If you look at his start or any starter, for the most part, you're talking 21 to 24 hitters," Dodgers manager Dave Roberts said. "That's kind of where guys are at, 21 to 24. So you kind of have an idea where guys are going to be and then you kind of layer in how they're throwing the baseball."

If that was his ration, Kershaw was burning through them in the first four innings.

For only the sixth time in his career (regular season or postseason), Kershaw allowed the leadoff batter to reach base in the first four innings of a start.

He danced out of trouble in the first two innings, but

Left fielder Joc Pederson tracks down a fly ball hit by Joey Wendle during the seventh inning of the Game 5 win. Pederson also hit a booming solo home run in the second inning, giving the Dodgers a 3-0 lead. (AP Images)

an infield single in the third was followed two batters later by a line drive down the right field line by Yandy Diaz. Betts moved to cut it off but took a flat route toward the ball and it skipped past him to the wall for an RBI triple. Diaz scored when Randy Arozarena singled through the left side of the Dodgers' infield.

But Arozarena was thrown out trying to steal second as Brandon Lowe struck out, ending the inning for Kershaw.

"Tonight, the whole night it was kind of a grind," he said. "I wasn't near as crisp as I was in Game 1. My slider really just wasn't as good as it was in Game 1 and my curveball, too, actually."

Back-to-back walks started the fourth inning with the Rays now trailing by just one, 3-2. Kershaw got a pop out and a strikeout (on his way to passing Justin Verlander to become the all-time postseason leader), bringing up Kevin Kiermaier.

The Rays made a calculation and decided Kiermaier's chances of driving in the run with two outs were less than a bold gamble — Manuel Margot tried to steal home, bolting as Kershaw reached his arms high over his head and paused in his distinctive delivery.

Muncy alerted him and Kershaw quickly threw home. Margot was called out. But the play was so close it went to replay review where squinting and rewinding and freeze-framing didn't change the call.

"That's happened to me before. I think it was Carlos Gomez with Houston and I think it was the same situation — two outs, trying to steal a run right there," Kershaw said. "I wasn't really anticipating it. But I have talked to first basemen in the past — Muncy, I've talked with him about it as well. 'Hey, I look at them originally but when I come set, I don't really see the runner, so you've got to yell at me if they start going.'"

The play actually settled Kershaw. He retired the side in order without a baserunner in the bottom of the fifth, striking out two, then retired the first two batters in the sixth — his sixth and seventh consecutive batters retired — each on one pitch.

But Lowe was batter No. 21 for Kershaw and, sure enough, Roberts came out of the dugout bound for the pitcher's mound. The Dodgers' infielders were more surprised than Kershaw and a roundtable discussion ensued.

"That's just one of those things where they talked about what was going to happen before that inning even started. That was the plan the whole time," Muncy said. "I think all of us wanted Kersh to stay in. But they had a plan and they executed the plan and it worked out for us."

Not before third baseman Justin Turner was caught by the Fox cameras and, even with rudimentary lip-reading skills, seeming to say, "I think he can get this (expletive)."

"Oh, it was Justin trying to lobby to keep him in the game," Roberts confirmed later. "You saw it right."

Roberts stayed the course he had set before the inning. Kershaw walked back to the dugout while the Dodger fans in attendance gave him an ovation. Roberts walked back to a cascade of boos.

"That was the plan," Kershaw said. "We talked about it before the inning. Even though it was just two pitches and made it seem super fast — you know, two outs and nobody on — we stuck with the plan. Credit to Doc for that one."

Those other scars October has inflicted on Kershaw often happened when the bullpen behind him poured acid all over the work he had done.

Not this time. Overamped in his previous World Series appearance, Dustin May was overpowering this time. He retired five of six batters, giving up a single to Kiermaier in the eighth before handing the ball to Victor Gonzalez with one out.

Gonzalez walked pinch-hitter Mike Brosseau to put the tying runs on base, but he retired the two most dangerous hitters in the Rays' lineup — Arozarena and Lowe. Returned to center field after his back tightness Saturday, Cody Bellinger came roaring in to snag Lowe's sinking liner and end the inning.

Having used rookies (May and Gonzalez) to get seven of the game's most pressure-packed outs, Roberts wasn't willing to ask another (Brusdar Graterol) to get the last three. He had two veterans to choose from — Blake Treinen and Kenley Jansen. Both had pitched in each of the previous two games.

"Kenley went two in a row. Blake went two in a row," Roberts said. "I just know we've done Blake three in a row more times. … So to feel that he can bounce back that third day is an easier bet for me."

Roberts still insists deposed closer Jansen is "a high-leverage guy." Treinen retired the side with little drama. ∎

Max Muncy watches his home run fly in the fifth inning of the win. The home run was his third of the postseason and gave the Dodgers a 4-2 lead that they wouldn't relinquish. (AP Images)

October 27, 2020 • Arlington, Texas
Dodgers 3, Rays 1

The Wait is Over!

Dodgers End World Series Title Drought After Come-From-Behind Win in Game 6
By Bill Plunkett

In a year that has been so improbable — for all of us — the possible finally happened.

Benefiting from a reverse Grady Little, the Dodgers rode a two-run burst in the sixth inning and an impeccable bullpen performance to a 3-1 victory in Game 6 of the World Series on Tuesday night at Globe Life Field.

The franchise that once made "Wait 'til next year" its unfortunate slogan for years has nothing more to wait for now. Tuesday's win came on the 16th anniversary of the Boston Red Sox ending their 86-year wait for a World Series title and ended a 32-year drought for the Dodgers that had them searching for their own curse to explain the annual disappointment.

"I've been saying World Series champs over and over again in my head just to see if it will sink in. So, no, I can't put it in words yet," said Clayton Kershaw, who charged in from the bullpen after the final out with the facial expression of a young "kiddo" on Christmas morning.

"I'm just so very grateful to be part of the team that is bringing back a World Series to Dodger fans after 32 years. They've waited a long time. To be on the team that did that in L.A. — you couldn't ask for anything more incredible."

In the last year of the Red Sox's drought, Little was run out of Boston after leaving Pedro Martinez in too long in Game 7 of the 2003 ALCS. The rabid talk radio audience

in … St. Petersburg, Fla., is not likely to run Rays manager Kevin Cash out of town. But his strict adherence to analytics might have cost the Rays a chance to extend this series to a winner-take-all Game 7.

The American League Cy Young Award winner in 2018 when he went 21-5 with a 1.89 ERA, Snell was that guy again Tuesday night with his team facing elimination.

Snell struck out the side in the first inning, retiring Mookie Betts, Corey Seager and Justin Turner on 12 pitches.

Through two innings, the only ball put in play was a checked-swing dribbler in front of home plate by Max Muncy. Chris Taylor led off the third inning with the Dodgers' first hit off Snell.

Taylor was stranded at second base and Snell went back to business, striking out the side again in the fourth and retiring the side in the fifth. Will Smith flew out to right field in that inning, only the second ball the Dodgers managed to hit out of the infield.

Through five innings, Snell had nine strikeouts and the Dodgers had failed to put a single one of Snell's fastballs in play.

"Had he stayed in the game, he may have pitched a complete game," Betts said. "He was pitching really, really well. That's the Cy Young Snell that came tonight. Once he came out of the game, it was a breath of fresh air."

Snell has been handled with care since surgery to

After 10 postseason berths and three World Series appearances, Clayton Kershaw raises his long-awaited World Series trophy. Kershaw was terrific in the World Series with a 2-0 record over 11-2/3 innings, a 2.31 ERA and 14 strikeouts. (AP Images)

remove bone chips from his pitching elbow in July 2019. So much care that he hadn't completed six innings since last July in his final start before the elbow surgery.

When Austin Barnes singled to center field with one out in the sixth inning, Cash adhered to established protocol — no third time through the lineup, no more for Snell even though the top three hitters in the lineup coming around again had gone 0 for 6 with six strikeouts against him.

"I was shocked," Dodgers outfielder Cody Bellinger said of Snell being pulled. "We were kind of joking around in the dugout — 'Way to go. We got him out in the sixth just like we wanted to do.' … Rallied from there. Snell had us stuck. He was gross. Yeah, I'd say it uplifted us."

The sigh of relief coming from the Dodgers' dugout nearly blew the roof at Globe Life Field open. Betts (unproductive all season against left-handed pitchers like Snell) doubled to left off right-handed reliever Nick Anderson. A wild pitch allowed Barnes to race home from third base and tie the score.

With Betts at third now, the Rays played the infield in and — unlike Game 1 before his game-turning dash home — third baseman Joey Wendle held Betts at third. No matter. When Seager bounced a ball to first baseman Ji-Man Choi, Betts bolted for home and beat Choi's throw with a head-first dive.

The play might replace Kirk Gibson's home run — or at least join it — on the highlight montage fans will see when they finally get to enter Dodger Stadium again.

"We have a certain formula with how we try to win ballgames, and it just didn't work out," Cash said of his decision to pull Snell.

Snell wouldn't criticize his manager, telling reporters after the game, "If you are going to write bad stories about the decision, he is usually right."

Dave Roberts knows all about those bad stories.

Cash's move to pull Snell was the kind of by-the-numbers move Dodgers fans accuse Roberts of making. Instead, Roberts was the one pushing all the right buttons at just the right time.

As pitcher Julio Urias (left) and catcher Austin Barnes begin to celebrate, the Dodgers rush the field to revel in the franchise's first championship since 1988. (AP Images)

After Tony Gonsolin gave up a first-inning home run to Randy Arozarena, Roberts didn't let him face the Rays' record-setting postseason threat again. He pulled the plug on Gonsolin after five outs, then toggled from Dylan Floro (struck out Arozarena) to Alex Wood (two spotless innings) through Pedro Baez (whew) to Victor Gonzalez and Brusdar Graterol and finally to Julio Urias.

That group combined to allow just two hits over the final 7-1/3 innings, first holding the line on the Rays' early lead then protecting the Dodgers' lead.

The Rays didn't advance a runner past first base against the Dodgers' bullpen. Betts added to the lead with a solo home run in the eighth inning, insurance as Urias retired the final seven Rays in order, setting off a dogpile 32 years in the making.

MLB couldn't escape coronavirus fears on the final night. Turner was removed from Game 6 before it ended because he received a positive COVID-19 test. The on-field celebration took place with the Dodgers wearing masks.

"It's a bittersweet night for us," MLB commissioner Manfred said in an on-field interview on FOX after the game. "We're glad to be done. I think it's a great accomplishment for our players to get the season completed, but obviously we're concerned when any of our players test positive. We learned during the game that Justin was a positive. He was immediately isolated to prevent spread."

On Twitter, Turner thanked those who reached out to him.

"I feel great, no symptoms at all. Just experienced every emotion you can possibly imagine. Can't believe I couldn't be out there to celebrate with my guys! So proud of this team & unbelievably happy for the City of LA," Turner wrote.

Turner would return to the field to celebrate with his teammates. ∎

Through ups, downs and an MLB season unlike any before it, the Dodgers captured the seventh World Series title in franchise history and shed the disappointment of 2017 and 2018. (AP Images)

Most Valuable Pest

Mookie Betts' Baserunning Puts the Dodgers Over the Top

By J.P. Hoornstra

Call Mookie Betts the World Series MVP: Most Valuable Pest.

The Dodgers' leadoff hitter made another heads-up play on the basepaths on Tuesday night, scoring the run that broke a 1-1 tie in the sixth inning on a routine ground ball to first base. It proved to be the winning run in the Dodgers' series-clinching 3-1 victory over the Tampa Bay Rays in Game 6 of the World Series.

Betts shot a double into the left field corner with one out against reliever Nick Anderson, sending Austin Barnes to third base. With an 0-and-1 count against the next hitter, Corey Seager, Anderson bounced a curveball in the dirt that got past catcher Mike Zunino. Barnes scored from third base, tying the score 1-1, and Betts advanced to third base on the wild pitch.

Seager hit a bouncing ground ball to Rays first baseman Ji-Man Choi on Anderson's next pitch. Betts broke for home plate on contact. He was halfway down the line by the time the ball got to Choi. By the time Zunino caught the relay throw, Betts' left hand was touching home plate at the end of a head-first slide.

Betts advanced two bases in the span of two pitches, neither one a hit, and the Dodgers turned a 1-0 deficit into a 2-1 lead they would not relinquish.

The Dodgers traded Alex Verdugo and two prospects for Betts, pitcher David Price, and cash in February. In July they signed him to a 12-year, $365 million contract extension. Without Betts, it's hard to imagine the Dodgers celebrating a championship today.

"I was traded to help get us over the hump," Betts said. "I used that as my fuel. Since Day One, that's obviously been the goal, to win a World Series. I'm just happy to be a part of it."

Betts provided his final World Series highlight with a solo home run in the eighth inning, his second of the series.

Baserunning might not get the most attention of Betts' five celebrated tools, but the Dodgers' leadoff hitter used his feet to disrupt one October game after another. There were seven stolen bases in the World Series. Betts had four of them.

"Stolen bases are a thing for me," Betts said after Game 1. "That's how I create runs and create havoc on the basepaths."

The 28-year-old outfielder led off the fifth inning of Game 1 by drawing a walk and stealing second base. Seager followed with a walk of his own, and the two pulled off a double-steal of second and third. The next batter, Max Muncy, hit a routine ground ball to first base. Betts broke on contact and beat Yandy Diaz's throw home.

The sequence — a mirror of the sixth inning of Game 6 — kicked off a four-run rally that turned a 2-1 Dodger lead into a 6-1 advantage.

By the end of the series, the Dodgers were champions for the first time since 1988, and Betts had a signature play all his own. He finished the six-game series with a .269 batting average (7 for 26), two home runs, three RBIs and five runs that made a tremendous difference in a tightly contested series.

"Coming in, when we acquired him, my expectations were sky high, and somehow he managed to find some headroom above that and exceed it," president of baseball operations Andrew Friedman said of Betts. "I can't say enough about the baseball player, the way he makes everyone around him better, and it's hard to imagine us sitting here without him." ∎

Mookie Betts reacts after scoring the go-ahead run in the sixth inning of the Game 6 victory, just one of many examples of Betts' heads-up baserunning in his first year with the Dodgers. (AP Images)

THE 2020 SEASON

Pasadena Star-News: Keith Birmingham

PRESIDENT OF BASEBALL OPERATIONS

Andrew Friedman

Dodgers' Andrew Friedman Went From Small-Market Wizard to Big-Market Mogul
By Bill Plunkett • May 20, 2019

The first time it really hit Andrew Friedman that he wasn't in Tampa anymore was Opening Day in 2015.

"Jimmy Rollins hits that big three-run home run and 50,000 people erupted," Friedman recalls now. "I took a minute and looked around and said, 'Wait a minute — I'm happy and 50,000 people are happy?' because I was used to being at Fenway or Yankee Stadium and when those crowds were happy, I was not. So it definitely set in."

There were other, quieter moments after Friedman "kind of took my professional snow globe and shook it up" by going from the small-market wizard who somehow got the Tampa Bay Rays into a World Series to a big-market mogul as the Dodgers' president of baseball operations — where he has built teams that have reached two more World Series.

"He and Farhan (Zaidi, GM during Friedman's first four seasons in L.A.) were sitting down with me in the office and something comes up about the competitive-balance tax, the CBT," Dodgers team president Stan Kasten says. "Andrew looks at Farhan and goes, 'Oh (shoot) — I think I have to learn those rules.' They had no idea about those rules. It was kind of funny that he had to learn different things.

"Never a factor in Tampa. Here, it's a factor."

During his years as the Rays' GM (2006-14), the team's entire player payroll never exceeded $76 million. During his first four years with the Dodgers, Friedman has already negotiated two different individual contracts worth more than that — Kenley Jansen's five-year, $80 million deal in 2016 and Clayton Kershaw's three-year, $93 million contract extension last fall. The Dodgers' payroll was the highest in baseball each of Friedman's first three seasons — breaking through that CBT each time.

"I enjoyed every minute of my time in Tampa Bay and loved the challenge. I had just reached a point in my career where I wanted to throw myself into the deep end in terms of having to re-think how I do my job," Friedman says. "Certain aspects would be important to maintain and other things I would have to re-wire how my brain processes different things."

As the Dodgers arrive in Tampa for a two-game interleague series against the Rays, some of that wiring is apparent — and some of it is unpopular with Dodger fans despite a .588 winning percentage since Rollins' homer and back-to-back National League pennants.

Any expectations that, unfettered from Tampa's financial restrictions, Friedman would behave like a shopaholic with a new credit card should have faded by now. In five offseasons, the Dodgers have spent to keep their own free agents but have only occasionally flirted with making a big-money commitment to bring in a free agent (such as Bryce Harper this past winter). The Dodgers' most expensive signing of a free agent from outside the organization has been A.J. Pollock, who could make $60 million over the next five seasons.

Instead, some of the Dodgers' most significant expenditures in the past five years have been what Friedman categorizes as "investment spending" — improving minor-league facilities and training staffs throughout the organization, dipping heavily into the international market

Andrew Friedman, President of Baseball Operations, walks past cutout pictures of Dodgers fans during the team's summer camp workout in preparation for the 2020 season. (Pasadena Star-News: Keith Birmingham)

and expanding the major-league support system, including new-age training tools like neuroscouting.

"We're big in everything — including on-field trainers and facilities," Kasten says. "You know, that first year we went really big in international. It hasn't always worked out. But the fact that you can stretch and do those things and not worry about the occasional misstep — that's a difference (from Tampa) in your prep, your mindset. I call those 'at the margins.'"

CUTTING EDGE

Under Friedman, the Rays were at the forefront of taking analytics from evaluation tool to a driving force in strategy with defensive shifts and lineup construction. That has spread quickly throughout the game and the Dodgers have assembled one of the deepest, most sophisticated (and influential) analytics departments.

"That competitive fire burns deep inside him," says Rays team president Matt Silverman, a good friend of Friedman. "No matter the setting, you can count on Andrew to try to outthink, outwork and outmaneuver the competition, and he inspires others around him to do the same."

There has been "bad investment" spending as well — dead money. Some of the biggest checks written in the past five seasons have been to players such as Carl Crawford, Scott Kazmir and Alex Guerrero when they were not playing for the Dodgers.

"Double-edged sword," Friedman says with a smile of the greater resources at his disposal in L.A.

Friedman gets high marks from players for his ability to connect personally — a failing of some in the wave of business-school products who have taken over front offices. Veteran infielder David Freese has played in four organizations and says "there's not a lot of guys like Andrew Friedman. He's unique." A pitcher in Tampa and now an assistant GM in the Dodgers' front office, Brandon Gomes says Friedman is "completely approachable" for players.

"I really appreciated the honesty he had with all the players," Gomes says. "As a player, you buy into that and feel like you can ask a question and it's not going to be judged in any way. It's a really good quality."

It's one that Friedman doesn't just put on for his walk-throughs in the clubhouse, according to Zaidi.

LEADERSHIP STYLE

"He does things in such a collaborative way that it never feels like he's imposing his will on a specific decision or particular area of the operation," Zaidi says. "That's really hard to do — kind of empowering people that way but still taking responsibility for the decisions and the path of the organization."

The challenge of managing limited resources has followed Friedman from Tampa to L.A. — but now it is time as much as money.

When he made the move west, Friedman had two sons, one 5 years old, the other not yet 3. A daughter was born in August 2015. During homestands, his wife, Robin, has often brought the kids to Dodger Stadium where they would soak up some dad time even slipping into their pajamas and brushing their teeth before Friedman would read them a bedtime story and send them home.

IMPACT REMAINS

Whatever magic Friedman practiced in Tampa seems to have lingered. The Rays won a surprising 90 games last season and come into the series with the Dodgers 10 games over .500 (27-17) and a half-game behind the New York Yankees in the American League East.

Friedman says he still follows the Rays when he can and roots for them — though not this week. But how much of his imprint remains on his former organization?

"I mean, he created the entire infrastructure they have right now," Zaidi says. "I'm certain he would deflect credit and give a lot of credit to (Rays GM) Erik Neander and (senior vice-president for baseball operations) Chaim Bloom and the job they have done — and they're certainly deserving of it.

"But I think as much as anything that organization and the way they make decisions and the way they think about baseball is unrecognizable from before he first got there. Just even creating, cultivating a culture of openness where the players embrace some of the less conventional, more innovative strategies that they employ — and employ successfully — is a big part of his legacy." ∎

Manager Dave Roberts confers with Andrew Friedman during a workout at Dodger Stadium prior to Game 1 of the National League Division Series. (Pasadena Star-News: Keith Birmingham)

5

SHORTSTOP

Corey Seager

Corey Seager Might Be a Forgotten Man in Dodgers' Loaded Lineup
By Bill Plunkett • February 20, 2020

The question catches Corey Seager off guard, like a ground ball taking an unexpected hop.

Do you think people have forgotten how good you are?

"I don't know how to answer that question," Seager says with a laugh. "Um, I don't really know. I mean, I don't think about that. I don't know that I've ever thought about that. My place is just to go out, compete and perform. Do what you can."

What Seager can do is pretty impressive. In his first two full big-league seasons (including his unanimous NL Rookie of the Year season in 2016), Seager won back-to-back Silver Slugger awards as the top offensive shortstop in the National League. He hit a combined .302 with an .867 OPS, 48 home runs and 73 doubles. In 2017, he was a Gold Glove finalist.

But then he disappeared for most of a season, undergoing surgery on his hip and his throwing elbow. Other heroes emerged in Los Angeles while he was rehabbing and last year's return to action came with tempered expectations.

During his first two seasons, Seager was entrenched as the Dodgers' No. 2 hitter, the modern era's home to a team's best hitter. Last season, he found himself dropped to the bottom half of the lineup, as low as seventh in some games.

It's enough to put a chip on a player's shoulder.

"I think every athlete has that in some way," Seager said. "How are you competitive if you don't have that?"

If Seager were so inclined, he has other reasons to feel slighted this spring. Once considered a foundational piece of the franchise's present and future, Seager's name was bandied about in trade rumors this offseason. The Dodgers' pursuit of Cleveland Indians shortstop Francisco Lindor seemed to make Seager expendable and there were reports of potential trade scenarios that would have sent Seager out of Los Angeles.

Seager admits he was "not bothered, maybe surprised is a better word" by those rumors.

"You understand the business side of it. You understand that," Seager said. "I didn't let it bother me. Everybody has their business point, the point where you realize it's a business and that was probably mine, you know? You understand that is part of the job you do.

"I try to stay out of it. I don't really read too much of that stuff. … You never know which one is real and which one is fake so why read it?"

It would have taken an awful lot to get Seager upset this winter. He was just happy to be out of the rehab world he inhabited following his surgeries. After going all-in on a dairy-free diet last year, his weight dipped into the 210s for the first time since high school. Now able to do

The 2020 season brought heavy expectations for Corey Seager following a 2019 spent rediscovering his form after multiple surgeries. Seager would go on to set the record for most postseason home runs by a shortstop. (Orange County Register: Kevin Sullivan)

a strengthening workout, not just a rehab plan (and wiser about his dietary options), the 6-foot-4 Seager is a lean 220 pounds again.

"It was nice," Seager said. "It was weird not waiting for something to heal to get started (working out). You just go, no restrictions. I didn't have to do any of that (physical therapy). It was like your brain had a load taken off.

"It's been more the mental part of it. To just not worry about it, having the confidence to know you can just go." ■

Above: Corey Seager takes batting practice during spring training workouts at Camelback Ranch in Phoenix. Opposite: Seager watches his single against the Chicago Cubs during their first spring training game, several months before the eventual start of the pandemic-shortened season. (Orange County Register: Kevin Sullivan)

35
CENTER FIELDER

Cody Bellinger

What Changes for Dodgers' Cody Bellinger Now That He Has an MVP Award?
By Bill Plunkett • March 5, 2020

I t is a life-changing achievement to win a Most Valuable Player award. But how does it really change your life?

"Got a little more money," Dodgers outfielder and 2019 National League MVP Cody Bellinger said, referring to the one-year, $11.5 million contract he signed this winter (the largest salary for any first-year arbitration-eligible player). "Other than that, my life hasn't changed at all."

It might. The MVP label brings with it certain expectations — like continuing to play at that level.

"He set a new benchmark for himself," Dodgers manager Dave Roberts said. "There's expectations always from the outside — whether it be from a team or individually. But I think that there's no more expectation a person puts on himself … than themselves.

"So I think for Cody it's kind of prepare the way he did and expect the results to be somewhat similar. He's an MVP player. I think that he's reached a certain plateau where I think he was pretty proud of himself. Now you got to kind of repeat it."

Mookie Betts has been through that. After leading the majors in batting average (.346), slugging percentage (.640), runs scored (129) and WAR (10.9) in 2018, he won the American League MVP award.

"Obviously opportunities come off the field," Betts said of the MVP aftermath. "Those are things that you can't really control, you can't do anything about. A lot of things change but it's not because you go out and try to make them change. People change around you.

"You may feel a little more pressure because you were an MVP and now have to back it up. But I think that's all from other people."

Whatever the reason, Betts' 2019 follow-up to his MVP season wasn't quite as good. He was hitting just .272 with a .467 slugging percentage at the All-Star break. And he admits some of that might have been internal pressure to match his 2018 numbers.

"Maybe a little," Betts said. "But I think 95 percent of it is outside your control. You guys will come in— and when I say you guys, I mean the media — if I go 0 for 20, then it's like, 'Oh, he lost it.' Instead of just — it's baseball."

Bellinger's breakout season in 2019 began early with a two-month tear at the start of the season. Through the Dodgers' first 50 games, Bellinger was batting .394 with 17 home runs and a 1.243 OPS.

It was an early statement of MVP status fueled by Bellinger's disappointment at being platooned at the end of the 2018 season (most bitterly in the World Series). That fire hasn't abated with the MVP honor, Roberts said.

"I just think that going into '19, into that winter, and all spring, everything he did there was more intent, more focused intent," Roberts said. "He took that all the way throughout the season, really, and it paid off. And I see that same kind of mindset again." ∎

Cody Bellinger struggled to match the staggering numbers of his 2019 MVP campaign, but he would prove invaluable with key contributions in 2020, such as his Game 7 go-ahead home run in the National League Championship Series. (Orange County Register: Kevin Sullivan)

Cody Bellinger celebrates with Max Muncy during a regular season game against the San Francisco Giants. (Los Angeles Daily News: David Crane)

'Holding Out Hope'

Dodgers Shut Down Training Complex in Arizona, Await Next Steps

By Bill Plunkett • March 20, 2020

The Dodgers have shut down their training complex in Arizona in response to the suggested precautions aimed at containing the coronavirus pandemic.

Organized workouts at the complex were shut down a week ago when Major League Baseball suspended spring training and postponed the start of the 2020 regular season. Dodgers manager Dave Roberts confirmed the complete shutdown of the facility during a radio interview on Friday.

Dodgers officials said the shutdown will last at least two weeks, at which point the team will re-assess the situation. A number of MLB teams have done the same.

"You're trying to be responsible and keep guys going that want to keep working and get treatment," Roberts said on "The Dan Patrick Show". "But I think ultimately you've got to be responsible and shutting down Camelback Ranch. … Taking care of the staff is the most important thing."

Roberts said he has been in contact with his players on a regular basis since the sport shut down last week.

"Every day it's a different group of players just to kind of catch up by way of text or call," he said.

Roberts said he is "trusting the fact that they're going to do whatever they can to stay in shape, keep their arms in shape, their bodies in shape."

"We don't know when this potential start date, if any, is going to happen. But I still can count on our guys," he said.

Roberts said he is still optimistic there will be a 2020 season of reasonable length, though he suspects there will have to be numerous "amendments" to scheduling and roster limits. He estimates a "two-, three-week ramp up" before games can begin "then some latitude for the roster size" to accommodate pitchers who won't be fully stretched out.

"Ideally, everyone wanted to get in that 162 (games) … or whatever that number," Roberts said. "But as every day goes on, the more we learn, it's seeming more unlikely. But I'm still holding out hope." ■

David Price, who joined the Dodgers in an offseason trade along with Mookie Betts, poses for a portrait during spring training in Phoenix. Along with several other players across the league, Price would later opt out of the 2020 season out of concern for his family's health. (Orange County Register: Kevin Sullivan)

MANAGER

Dave Roberts

Dave Roberts 'Excited' But Cautious About Dodgers 2020 Season
By Bill Plunkett • June 24, 2020

Dave Roberts followed the often-disheartening back and forth between MLB's owners and its players' union, read all the discussion of what adjustments the sport would have to make in the midst of a pandemic and worried about the news of coronavirus outbreaks among players and staff with multiple teams.

But when the news came down earlier this week that baseball would be back — next week for training camps, July 23 and 24 for real, live but fan-free games — his reaction was natural and simple.

"Excitement. I'm excited," the Dodgers manager said Wednesday. "I'm certainly excited to get back to playing. But I'm also sensitive to what's happening in our country and in our state here in California. I'm confident we're going to do everything we can to keep everybody healthy. There are some people that are more concerned than others. We've got to continue to be mindful of that.

"But I think on the baseball side it'll be good to get back to playing."

For three months, Roberts' only contact with his players has been through texts, phone or Zoom calls. His coaching staff has been in more frequent contact, having split the roster into sections. Roberts plans a "Zoom team meeting" with the full squad later this week after the logistics of "spring training 2.0" are finalized.

A "handful" of Dodgers at a time have been using Dodger Stadium for workouts including some live batting practice sessions where hitters could face pitchers. The same was true at Camelback Ranch until the outbreak of positive tests at multiple training complexes prompted MLB to order all complexes shut down in Arizona and Florida. All of that has players "right where they need to be" at this point, Roberts said.

Once that preseason training camp starts next week, the Dodgers will likely use an alternate site in addition to Dodger Stadium in order to spread out the 60 players expected to report. When the season begins, rosters will be expanded — 30 players for the first 15 days, 28 players through the first four weeks then 26 for the rest of the season — with a taxi squad of players working out at an alternate site in case they are needed to replace injured players (or positive coronavirus test cases).

The Dodgers have a likely second site available in Rancho Cucamonga, usually home to their Class-A affiliate.

Roberts said the recent news of players testing positive for the coronavirus doesn't curb his excitement about forging ahead with a 2020 season, but it provides "a wakeup call" reminding everyone how serious the situation is.

"I know specifically with the Dodgers what we're trying to do and how seriously we've taken it from the beginning," he said. "I just think it's a wake-up call for

After months of corresponding with his team through calls and texts, manager Dave Roberts was enthusiastic and optimistic about the 2020 season. (Orange County Register: Kevin Sullivan)

anyone that doesn't think they can be affected — even if you are in peak condition. So when the organization doesn't have eyes on you going forward to really take it seriously because it could affect the entire industry. One thing that cannot happen is for us to start and then have to stop because of a breakout in Major League Baseball."

The 60-game regular season leaves little room for error in many ways. A year ago, the Dodgers were 41-19 after 60 games, already nine games up in the NL West. Two years ago, however, they were just 30-30, sitting in third place.

"I think the thing that worries me is any team can get off to a slow start and you just don't have the time to recover. I think it's really important," Roberts said. "If anything, the unknown is kind of how we get off to a good start. I'm not really concerned about the mindset. I'm not really concerned about the injury piece because I love our depth. I just think you've still got to go out there and get off to a good start."

As the NBA has prepared for its attempted restart of the 2020 season, some players have decided to opt out rather than take the health risk for themselves or their families.

Because of a heart condition which has required two surgical procedures, Dodgers closer Kenley Jansen is considered at high risk during the pandemic. He could opt out and still receive his pro-rated salary for 2020. Dodgers reliever Scott Alexander is diabetic. But Roberts said none of his players have given him any indication that they would do the same.

Reliever Joe Kelly did an interview with a Boston radio station this week and said he had "thought about it" and discussed it with his wife. In the end, he said he felt obligated to his teammates to play.

"For me, if any player chooses to opt out because they feel they're at risk and potentially could put their family at risk, I support them 100 percent," Roberts said. "But no one has given me any indication.

"I think everybody has their own decision to make." ∎

Dave Roberts wears a face mask in the Dodger Stadium dugout before a game against the Los Angeles Angels. (Pasadena Star-News: Keith Birmingham)

Dodger For Life

Mookie Betts Signs 12-year Extension with Dodgers, Biggest in MLB History

By Bill Plunkett • July 22, 2020

Just last week, Dodgers manager Dave Roberts admitted to a valid fear — shared with many fans (and even analysts) — when he acknowledged "there were numerous times over the last few months I wondered if we'd ever see" Mookie Betts play a game in a Dodgers uniform.

Before Betts even plays that first official game as a Dodger (Thursday's delayed season opener), that fear has been put to rest. Roberts and everyone else can look forward to seeing Betts in a Dodgers uniform for years to come after the Dodgers announced that they had signed Betts to a 12-year contract extension Wednesday.

The deal could keep the 27-year-old Betts in Dodger blue through the 2032 season when he will be 39 years old.

The contract will take effect beginning in 2021 and reportedly pay Betts $365 million, making it the most lucrative contract in Dodgers history and the most lucrative extension in baseball history (surpassing Mike Trout's $360 million deal with the Angels, though that was a 10-year deal). Betts will make $10 million this season (the prorated portion of his $27 million 2020 salary), making his commitment to the Dodgers a 13-year, $375 million arrangement.

"When you're making an investment of this magnitude, you're not just betting on the player's ability," Dodgers president of baseball operations Andrew Friedman said. "You're also betting on the person, and with that we couldn't be more comfortable to make that bet than on Mookie Betts.

"Obviously, he's an extraordinary talent. Mookie can impact the game in every facet. But I think what's really stood out to us in our couple months of being around him, it's just the work ethic, the burning desire to get better on a daily basis. I think the tone that he will set with that standard for our young players that are in our clubhouse now and also the ones that come up in the future will leave an indelible mark on this organization so you couldn't be more excited."

This 13-year marriage is the product of a whirlwind courtship.

The Dodgers traded for Betts (and David Price) on the eve of spring training, having swung and missed (to varying degrees) on attempts to give mega-million dollar contracts to free agents Bryce Harper, Gerrit Cole or Anthony Rendon over the past two winters and survived a near breakdown of the deal with the Boston Red Sox.

They knew full well at the time that Betts could be a free agent this fall and had already turned down a 10-year, $300 million offer from the Red Sox.

"That's a good question," Friedman said when asked what he thought the odds of re-signing Betts were at the time of the trade. "I knew how strong our commitment was.

"I was hopeful that we would make a good impression on Mookie just with the communication and the people we have and just the culture that's been created that Doc had done such a good job of creating in the clubhouse. I think that's something you can tell right away. And so we were hopeful that he would get here and fall in love with

Mookie Betts celebrates with DJ Peters after hitting an RBI sacrifice fly during the Dodgers' spring training home opener, Betts' first game in a Dodgers uniform. (Orange County Register: Kevin Sullivan)

it. We'd go out, late March, Opening Day, win a bunch of games, win the World Series and we'd end up kind of staying together."

The Dodgers had barely five weeks to make that impression — in Arizona, not Los Angeles — before the sport was shut down and players scattered, waiting out a quarantine that will delay the start of the season four months.

Friedman said there had been some contract discussions in March but "obviously, the world kind of changed on us, which put things on hold for a while." Talks resumed "five, six days ago" with Betts requesting that discussions end before the season started.

Despite the limited exposure to the culture Friedman boasted about, Betts opted to make a long-term commitment to his new home.

"I think just being here, the time I've been here, the people here made me feel so comfortable," said Betts who spent the quarantine at his home in Tennessee, fishing, golfing and spending time with his 21-month old daughter.

"The talent all up and down from the minor leagues, everybody in the front office from the owner on down is amazing. I think this organization is a well-oiled machine. I love it. I'm super, super excited to be a part of it for the next 12, 13 years — however many years it is. … I gotta bring some rings back to LA, for sure."

Betts' use of the plural "rings" brought to mind LeBron James' famous proclamation of multiple championships — "not one, not two, not three …" after taking his talents to Miami. Betts laughed off the comparison.

"I gotta be Mookie Betts. I can't be LeBron," he said with a smile that should become very familiar to Dodgers fans over the next 13 years.

Betts joins the Dodgers as a four-time All-Star, four-time Gold Glove winner and three-time Silver Slugger with the potential to become just the second player (after Frank Robinson) to win an MVP award in both leagues — and a strong endorsement from one of his new neighbors.

"I'm excited for him. Shot him a text earlier," Angels outfielder Mike Trout said Wednesday afternoon. "Being so close to him now, it's pretty cool to have him out here.

"Playing against him in Boston, was a teammate at a couple of All-Star Games — what a great person. I've never heard anything bad about him. … His game is unbelievable. I love how he plays. You never see him upset, always playing the game with passion, always smiling and always putting up big numbers every year."

There was some question about the salary numbers Betts could have put up this winter as a free agent in uncertain times. Teams are taking a financial hit with an abbreviated season in 2020 with the potential for depressed revenues again in 2021 if fans are still unable to attend games. A Collective Bargaining Agreement that will expire following next season added another unknown.

Betts did reportedly get some protection, receiving a $65 million signing bonus and accepting low salaries ($17.5 million in 2021 and 2022) up front. A large portion of the salary is deferred for now and there are apparently no opt-outs or no-trade provisions.

"From our standpoint back in March, if you would have said, 'Hey Mookie wants to sign just a two-year contract. He just wants to sign for 2021 and 2022' — what we would have done in March and what we would do now would be very different," Friedman said.

"But I think from ownership on down, this just speaks to the faith we have in things getting back to normal. Obviously this is over a much longer period of time which helps in that confidence. And it's really high once we kind of get through this. And fortunately, when you go 12 years you have nothing but time." ∎

Only months after joining the Dodgers in an offseason trade with the Red Sox, Mookie Betts felt comfortable with the organization, opting to sign a 12-year extension before the start of the season. (Orange County Register: Kevin Sullivan)

11
LEFT FIELDER

A.J. Pollock

Parenthood Changed Dodgers' A.J. Pollock, and It's Been Good for His Game
By Bill Plunkett • August 6, 2020

A.J. Pollock had an awful lot on his plate over the past several months. A lot of it had nothing to do with baseball.

Maddi Mae Pollock was born on March 19, arriving three months premature and setting off a 130-day stress test for her parents of "home-hospital, home hospital," as A.J. put it. In June, the anxiety was ratcheted even higher for the first-time father when he contracted COVID-19 and had to quarantine at home for most of two weeks, staying away from both Maddi and his wife, Kate.

By the time baseball returned in July, it was no longer the most important thing in Pollock's life.

"I've always had teammates who had a baby," Pollock said recently after Maddi was discharged from the neonatal intensive care unit. "They got to go home, and their wife was pregnant, they see the baby and they go back. It was a pretty planned and structured deal.

"For us, I had to go back (to Arizona). I had to learn a lot of things from the doctors before they let her go. We had to get some things in order at the house. She still has a feeding tube in, so I had to learn how to work that. She ripped that out once while I was there. That was not fun, holding a baby down while Kate worked that through her nose.

"Baseball, it consumes a lot of your mental stamina. Most of your day, you're thinking about baseball. This completely put that aside."

The altered priorities have been good for Pollock so far. Despite arriving to summer workouts late because of his COVID-19 illness, he has started the season 12 for 37 (.324) with four doubles, three home runs and team-highs in slugging percentage (.676) and OPS (1.051) in 11 games.

"I'm learning a lot now," Pollock said. "Baseball's been my life. It's been my life for so long and it's always gonna be a huge part of who I am. … I put a lot of work into baseball and I think there's a point where you're just kind of overdoing it.

"So maybe, yeah, maybe it's just an eye-opener to put in your work and then go home and enjoy being at home. I've tried to do that (before) but obviously it's not as easy as just the words there. I think this has kind of forced me to just — I have to go home. I have to help Kate out because she is very overwhelmed, dealing with a little newborn the whole day, a preemie newborn the whole day. So I have to turn that switch off. I have to flip that switch off and be a dad at home. So I think it's been eye-opening for me, for sure."

Another first-time father, Mike Trout, has furthered the case for dad strength this week with a home run in his first at-bat after rejoining the Angels following the birth of his first child — and three homers in his first seven at-bats as a dad.

"I do think it can be a good thing," said father of two and Dodgers manager Dave Roberts, talking about the changed perspective parenthood brings. "You certainly

With cardboard cutouts of fans in the background, A.J. Pollock takes an at-bat against the Los Angeles Angels. (Pasadena Star-News: Keith Birmingham)

miss out on some sleep. But it's a good kind of loss of sleep to see what a blessing it is to have a child especially what he had to go through with Maddi being born premature. So I definitely think that's a good thing."

There have been physical changes as well. Roberts points to Pollock being "synced up" mechanically at the plate, thanks at least in part to his relationship with hitting coach Robert Van Scoyoc (who worked for the Diamondbacks briefly before joining the Dodgers last year). And Roberts says he sees benefits in Pollock having dropped weight heading into this season.

"I think the first thing I saw this summer camp was he's a lot lighter," Roberts said. "Talking to A.J. last year, he wanted to put on weight, to get stronger. And so I think he's lighter. His foot speed, he's faster this year."

Maddi's long hospital stay wasn't the first medical issue for the Pollock family. Her father cannot be evaluated without touching on his history of injuries. The pandemic has done him a favor in that regard — for the first time since 2015, Pollock got through April, May, June and July without going on the injured list.

"Injuries are tough. It's part of the game," Pollock said. "Definitely you want to be healthy, you want to be out there, you want to be able to contribute every day. In baseball you just get in this rhythm. You get to the field. You get your routines. You play and when you get injured everyone else stays in this rhythm and you're thrown out of the rhythm.

"If you have to be injured and you have to rehab, you try to get better and adapt. But obviously if you can stay on the field and stay in the flow it's much easier, for sure."

Now Maddi has forced Pollock to adapt in other ways, forcing him to accept a new work-life balance.

"I think I just show up at the ballpark and get my work in and if it's not a good day you just kind of flush it," he said. "It's simple but obviously for me it's not that easy to do. When you have a bad game, you're thinking about a little bit. In this situation, I leave it on the field and then I go home and enjoy being with my wife and my daughter.

"It's kind of a little eye-opening for me, kind of just playing a little free and easy. I can't explain it. It's obviously only been 11 games but so far so good." ∎

A.J. Pollock scores off of a double by Corey Seager during a game against the Colorado Rockies at Dodger Stadium. (Los Angeles Daily News: David Crane)

Carrying the Lesson Forward

Dodgers Coach George Lombard Tries to Honor the Work of His Activist Mother

By J.P. Hoornstra • June 12, 2020

The Federal Bureau of Investigation monitored the mother of Dodgers coach George Lombard over parts of nine years. The dossier on Posy Lombard is 313 pages long. It's a page-turner.

The Ku Klux Klan tried to thwart her from demonstrating in Mississippi in 1965 (page 96). She was suspected of abetting an accused terrorist in 1969 (page 224). In April 1974, around the time Hank Aaron was breaking Babe Ruth's home run record, the FBI was still gathering intel on Lombard's various political affiliations in Atlanta (page 219).

Today we would call Posy Lombard a civil rights activist, a kindred spirit to those who marched when George Floyd died at the hands of a Minneapolis police officer on May 25. History renders its verdict on its own schedule. Longtime FBI director J. Edgar Hoover believed Lombard warranted a letter to the Secret Service, calling attention to her "conduct or statements indicating a propensity for violence and antipathy toward good order and government" (page 238).

There's more. A lot more. All of it points to something George Lombard has been able to piece together for himself over the years: his mom was a woman ahead of her time.

"That's where I need to be more educated, and just kind of learn more from what was happening during that time," he said.

Easier said than done. Posy Lombard died in an automobile accident when George was 10 years old. The same woman who heard Martin Luther King speak at the Lincoln Memorial in 1963 was already a mother when George was born in 1975. By the time he was old enough to understand the rarity of her life's path, she was gone.

Somewhere in Posy Lombard's file as an activist lies a lesson or two for today. It might be incredibly useful to someone holding the megaphone that comes with a major league uniform, in the midst of a national conversation about civil rights.

Carrying that lesson forward? That's heavy.

ENCOUNTER WITH THE KKK

Start with something familiar — a story nominally about baseball.

It's 1965. Posy Lombard was 21 years old, a recent graduate of Smith College in Massachusetts. That summer, she was working in Natchez, Miss., as a volunteer with the Council of Federated Organizations (COFO), an activist group focused on civil rights. When

Dodgers first base coach George Lombard has worked to honor and carry forward the activist legacy of his mother, Posy Lombard, a prolific civil rights organizer. (Pasadena Star-News: Keith Birmingham)

the FBI began surveilling Lombard's activity with COFO, her goal was simple: to help integrate a segregated public park in Natchez.

The COFO group was a mix of black and white, of college-educated northerners and local kids fighting for their own liberties. Many of them lived out of a four-bedroom house in town called the "Freedom House." Volunteers cooked there, ate there, and slept there. They held workshops on nonviolent resistance. They wrote "freedom songs." Their ends were lofty and their means were quaint, but enough to arouse attention.

Ferriday, La., is a couple towns over from Natchez, on the other side of the Mississippi River. There, a different group was agitating for civil rights under the CORE (Congress Of Racial Equality) banner. When Posy Lombard was in Natchez, the CORE home was nearly fire-bombed. Its six members took refuge in the Freedom House. If danger wasn't omnipresent, it was never far away.

On the afternoon of July 18, five cars carrying COFO members set out from the Freedom House to Duncan Park in Natchez. They brought "sports equipment," Lombard would tell the FBI later, "to play games if we got into the park." Their plan was thwarted.

Two days earlier, a tipster had alerted the Natchez police that COFO was planning a "demonstration." The police chief alerted the mayor. The mayor ordered the Duncan Park golf course to stay open but closed both its swimming pools — the white pool and the black pool. Someone alerted the KKK. According to a witness statement provided to the FBI, signs were posted near Duncan Park indicating the Klan planned a baseball game for the same time as the demonstration.

Somewhere during the mile-and-a-half drive to Duncan Park, the COFO caravan was cut off by a green Mercury Comet station wagon. At the park entrance, the car mysteriously stalled. A local Klan leader arrived at the scene, and the two men parked their cars side-by-side. "I did see two men up near this green car which had blocked our lane of traffic," Posy Lombard told the FBI. "One of them handed the other an object that I believe was a small pistol."

Fortunately, the standoff ended peacefully. The COFO caravan turned around and drove back to the Freedom House. The Klan dispersed. The next day, seven COFO members drove back to Duncan Park. They played on the playground, then drove home.

WHAT TO DO WITH WHITE PRIVILEGE

To understand what "white privilege" looks like, study the maternal line of George Lombard's family tree. His grandfather, the late George Francis Fabyan Lombard, was a senior associate dean and professor of human relations at Harvard Business School.

One distant relative was the governor of Iowa. Another relative sailed to America on the Mayflower.

When Posy Lombard headed south, she turned her back on this birthright. Her record proves it: she was arrested in 1965 for "disobeying a police officer" in Montgomery, and for trespassing in Tuscaloosa in 1967. George Lombard said his mother was jailed "probably seven to 10 times" in all. Her phone was wiretapped in Birmingham, and possibly in Atlanta. The FBI tracked her every move at home and abroad, including visits to Cuba, Bulgaria and Liberia. By the time George was born, the bureau had collected its last report on Posy.

One lesson for today, perhaps, is that Posy Lombard never left. While the fight against Jim Crow faded from the national consciousness and the FBI's secret spotlight, it remained her cause. She raised her three children on a three-acre plot of land in a rough part of Southeast Atlanta. They had goats and chickens and cows. Their nearest neighbors were close friends of the family, George Lombard said, and they shared an eccentric existence.

"When we were young, everyone we hung out with was biracial," he said. "It was normal to see other people who looked like me."

One excerpt from Posy Lombard's FBI dossier (page 269) hints at her worldview: "Source described Posey (sic) as a person who believed that the white persons (sic) place in the civil rights movement is to work against racism in white communities and indicated she was a full time organizer in the white community of Atlanta, Georgia."

BRINGING THE LESSON HOME

George Lombard does not benefit from white privilege. His father, Paul Williams, is a dark-skinned African American man. In 1998, when he debuted with the Braves, George Lombard would have been counted among the 14.3 percent of major league players who identified as African American. (That figure had sunk to 8.2 percent by 2008, when Lombard played his final exhibition game with the Dodgers.)

Lombard lives with his wife and two sons near Miami in the offseason. Earlier this month he was visiting a friend's house, which is currently under construction on the waterfront.

"The house is open. They haven't put in windows and doors," he said. "We get back from going out and hanging out with them. I said, 'Let's go check out Carlos's house.' I told his son, 'Brixton, why don't you come with me? I don't feel comfortable going there myself' — without even thinking. Your mind automatically thinks like that. It shouldn't. I just said it because it's my natural reaction."

Lombard knows the story of Ahmaud Arbery, a black man who was fatally shot after visiting a construction site while he was jogging in rural Georgia in February. The cases of Arbery and Floyd sparked a nationwide reckoning. All 30 major league teams, as well as the league itself, recently released statements condemning racism.

Last Friday, about a dozen Dodger coaches joined in a Zoom call. Lombard recommended bringing in a professional leadership consultant, Lucas Jadin, to facilitate the uncomfortable but necessary conversations about race and empathy the moment demands.

"I got pretty emotional on the call with our staff," Lombard said. "I was feeling guilty because I haven't done enough. I'm going to be better at taking stances because I do have a voice. The coaching staff does have a voice. I need to get more educated on everything that's going on in the world."

FINDING HIS VOICE

A short time after Farhan Zaidi called to offer him the Dodgers' first-base coach's job in December 2015, Lombard got a call from the University of Phoenix:

He had passed his final class. He had completed his bachelor's degree in psychology. But having a college education and being Posy Lombard's son cannot imbue courage by themselves.

George Lombard had never spoken publicly about his mother's legacy until this year. His cousin, Louisa Lombard, is a professor at Yale University. She invited Lombard to visit the New Haven campus in January. There, he spoke to a group of about 80 students, then met with some of the baseball coaches and players.

The surge of civil rights protests helped Lombard further his voice. On June 3, he participated in a Zoom call with a national network of high school athletic directors. Wednesday, he was the featured Zoom speaker in the Los Angeles Dodgers Foundation's "Virtual Coaches Training Series." He is suddenly among the most in-demand speakers in baseball.

Globally, Lombard's speaking career is a small drop in a large bucket of cultural revelations. In baseball, it represents something more: the potential to tell a story too expansive for the first base coach's box at Dodger Stadium. Telling it required time, and perspective, and tragedy. When he first approached Jadin about finding his voice as a leader, Lombard said Jadin asked him a simple question: What do you want people to know about you?

"The coolest thing," Lombard said, "is my mom's story." ■

Making a Statement

Dodgers, Giants Postpone Their Game in Wake of Jacob Blake Shooting

By J.P. Hoornstra • August 26, 2020

Dodgers right fielder Mookie Betts awoke Wednesday expecting to play a baseball game against the San Francisco Giants. A national conversation was on his mind, too. After he arrived at Oracle Park, the conversation was on Betts' phone.

Jacob Blake, a Black man, was shot by a White police officer in his hometown of Kenosha, Wisconsin, on Sunday. Protests ensued across the country. The Milwaukee Bucks decided not to play a playoff game Wednesday against the Orlando Magic. The Milwaukee Brewers opted against playing the Cincinnati Reds.

Betts, who is Black, was exchanging text messages with members of his family. By Wednesday afternoon, he had decided to sit out the game against the Giants.

Soon Betts was not alone. The Dodgers met for more than an hour in the visitors' clubhouse in San Francisco. They listened to Betts' reasons for sitting out. They exchanged ideas as a group. They talked to players on the Giants' side.

By 6 p.m., less than an hour before the scheduled first pitch, it was official: The Dodgers weren't playing. The game was being postponed. It was one of three games called off on a day of protest around Major League Baseball.

"Hopefully this is the first step to change," Betts said.

The Brewers and Cincinnati Reds were the first to decide to postpone their game Wednesday. The Seattle Mariners and San Diego Padres followed. Several Black and White baseball players — including Matt Kemp, Jason Heyward, Dexter Fowler and Jack Flaherty — also made the individual choice to sit out their scheduled games.

Dodgers manager Dave Roberts, the son of a Black father and Japanese mother, said he would not have managed Wednesday's game had it been played.

"To not play, allowing us to use our platform, to use our voices, and to let the world know, the country know, how sad, frustrated and angry we all are, that looking at the world, the way the country is right now, people are being treated this way — people of color," Roberts said. "These conversations need to be had."

The Dodgers and Giants will make up the game by playing a doubleheader — two seven-inning games — on Thursday.

"If Mookie plans on playing, I think we're going to play," pitcher Clayton Kershaw said.

Kershaw was scheduled to start Wednesday's game. After George Floyd was killed at the hands of a Minneapolis police officer in May, the former Most Valuable Player became an outspoken advocate for racial injustice.

Though he was the only White person on a Zoom

The scoreboard at Oracle Park in San Francisco reads "Black Lives Matter" while the field remains empty after the Giants and Dodgers elected to sit out their contest as part of a day of protest across sports. (AP Images)

call with reporters Wednesday, Kershaw did not appear out of place standing beside Betts, Roberts and pitcher Kenley Jansen.

"More than anything, as a teammate of Mookie's, as a member of this team with (Roberts) and George (Lombard, the Dodgers' first base coach) and (strength and conditioning coach Travis Smith), as a White player on this team, how can we show support?" Kershaw asked. "We felt the best thing to do was support them by not playing."

The game was scheduled to air nationally on ESPN. By sitting it out, the Dodgers made a visible statement. It was not their first.

All Dodger players wore a "Black Lives Matter" patch on their Opening Day jerseys, then auctioned them off with proceeds to benefit the California Funders for Boys & Men of Color Southern California: Our Kids, Our Future Fund. Betts knelt during the playing of the national anthem before the July 23 game at Dodger Stadium.

In July, Kershaw, Joc Pederson, Ross Stripling and Justin Turner joined leaders of the Brotherhood Crusade, the Children's Defense Fund of California, the Community Coalition, and the Brothers, Sons, Selves Coalition in a listening session.

Roberts' remarks Wednesday were his strongest yet on the issue of social justice.

"There's no bigger issue right now," he said. "It's not a political issue. I understand there's an election coming up, but this is a human being issue. We all need to be treated the same way. A Black man being shot seven times in the back … that just can't happen."

Roberts said he had the support of Dodgers chairman Mark Walter and the team's front office if the game were played without him.

Lombard, the son of a Black father and White mother, might have chosen to continue his own form of protest by wearing black shoes in the first base coach's box.

"We just need to get everybody's attention," Lombard said. "I don't know if people know the right way to handle the situation, but the only way these issues are going to get

solved is to talk about them, to find out why these things continue to happen."

Major League Baseball issued a statement of its own Wednesday: "Given the pain in the communities of Wisconsin and beyond following the shooting of Jacob Blake, we respect the decisions of a number of players not to play tonight. Major League Baseball remains united for change in our society and we will be allies in the fight to end racism and injustice."

For Betts, what might have been a mournful occasion turned into a powerful team-bonding exercise. In July, he signed a 12-year contract worth $365 million— the longest and most lucrative deal in Dodger history. He was already destined to become the face of the franchise.

Wednesday, Betts added a powerful voice to a national conversation that has nothing to do with baseball.

"I was already tight with everyone in the clubhouse," he said, "but now that I know everybody has my back more than I already thought means a lot. I'll always remember this day and I'll always remember this team having my back." ■

Mookie Betts kneels during the national anthem on opening day. Betts has been a prominent voice among players in addressing systemic racial injustice, and he gained the support of his teammates, who joined him in protest later in the season. (AP Images)

22
STARTING PITCHER

Clayton Kershaw

Clayton Kershaw Hasn't Turned Back the Clock — But He Has Turned Up the Speed
By Bill Plunkett • August 20, 2020

Clayton Kershaw has not found a way to turn back time. But he has found a way to recover some of what it took away.

Through his first four starts this season, the Dodgers ace has reversed a four-year slide in his fastball velocity, regaining two miles per hour on the pitch. He averaged over 91.5 mph in each of his first three starts — the first time he has held that much velocity for three consecutive starts since his first three outings in the 2018 season — before falling just short with an average velocity of 91.425 mph against the Seattle Mariners Thursday.

Against the Angels last week (when he allowed just one hit in seven innings), Kershaw's fastball averaged 92.5 mph — the highest it has been in a single start since the 2017 World Series.

"(Velocity) is not everything. But I knew it was in there. So I think that's what's frustrating," Kershaw said after the start in Anaheim.

"These last couple years, it's been hard to figure out why it hasn't been coming out the way I want it to. Obviously, you grind and try to make good starts and stuff like that. We threw a lot of different things at it — our strength and conditioning guys, training staff, offseason stuff. Everybody did a great job with me, trying to figure out what works, what doesn't work. I can't pinpoint one

specific thing. But all the things we've tried, there's a lot of things that have stuck. It is gratifying, for sure."

Kershaw has been reluctant to talk about his visit to Driveline Academy last fall. The facility relies on sophisticated analytics to bring out more velocity in pitchers — Kenley Jansen and Alex Wood have also recovered velocity after visits to Driveline last offseason — and its devotees use a variety of weighted-ball exercises to improve arm strength. Kershaw could be seen doing the exercises during spring training in Arizona.

Pitching coach Mark Prior gives the 32-year old Kershaw credit for being open-minded enough to look for answers.

"Over time as we get older and he puts more miles on his body pitching, the body starts changing. Things start tightening. Things start loosening," Prior said, aware of the history of back problems that has characterized Kershaw's aging. "I think he was able to do some different things and attack it from a 360-degree approach to unlock some of the body to allow his arm to deliver the velocity that he was accustomed to.

"I don't think that's anything that's unusual for veteran pitchers especially guys that have been around for a decade to have to go out and … figure out where their body is in their 30s than it is in their young 20s. He spent a lot of time trying to figure out the right steps and the

Clayton Kershaw visited Driveline Academy as part of his offseason training, which may be responsible for an uptick in velocity during the 2020 season. (Orange County Register: Kevin Sullivan)

right things to do and now he's seeing the dividends — in the velocity and in the command too."

The added velocity gives Kershaw more "margin for error," Prior said and also makes his slider more effective.

"Obviously the slider for him … when it's good, it's hard and it's short and it basically just misses barrels," Prior said. "I think that's the other component. Now is the velocity the same on the slider even when his velocity is down? Sometimes it is. But I don't think the movement and the sharpness of the bite is the same. That's kind of the added benefit. Yes, it gives him some room on his fastball. But I think the arm speed also helps him lock in his really good slider." ∎

Above: Clayton Kershaw high fives teammate Mookie Betts after defeating the Milwaukee Brewers and taking the National League Wild Card series. Opposite: Kershaw pitches in the decisive Game 2 of the Wild Card match-up. (Pasadena Star-News: Keith Birmingham)

50

RIGHT FIELDER

Mookie Betts

Dodgers Marvel at Mookie Betts' Everyday Excellence
By Bill Plunkett • October 22, 2020

Mookie Betts finished second to Mike Trout in the voting for the American League MVP Award in 2016.

There was no shame in that. After all, Mike Trout wins the award every year, or seems to, and has been acclaimed as the greatest player of his generation, one of the best in baseball history.

Betts had just finished his second full season in the big leagues with the Boston Red Sox. He received nine first-place votes (to Trout's 19) following a season that saw him make his first All-Star Game.

But at age 23, Betts knew it wasn't enough. He didn't want that to be all he was.

"I think back in 2016 once I came in second in the MVP, I knew it was going to be tough for me to repeat that or get better," Betts said. "I told myself I just wanted to be consistent. Watching the greats play, they're all just really consistent. They hit their home runs constantly. They drive in runs constantly. Walk constantly. Make good plays constantly. It's not just one and then a long period of time before another one.

"You just have to be good at all aspects of the game all the time. Don't take plays off. And I think 2016 was when I told myself that's what I wanted to do."

Two years later, it was Betts who won the AL MVP award and Trout who finished second.

The drive that fueled that desire to be "good at all aspects of the game all the time" and the player it produced are what has most impressed the Dodgers in their first season as Betts' baseball home.

"Mookie's pretty special. He just does things on the baseball field that not a lot of people can do and he does it so consistently, which I think separates him from a lot of guys," said Clayton Kershaw, another elite-level competitor driven to separate himself from a lot of guys.

"I think it's just the baserunning, the consistency of everything he does. The defense. He does some special things like hit homers, take the extra base and things like that. I think the day-in, day-out consistency of what he does on the baseball field separates him. I mean, you might see one game and not really appreciate Mookie to his full potential but now that we've seen him for – well, COVID-shortened but a full season for us – you kind of get to appreciate it on a day-in, day-out basis now."

No sport demands day-in, day-out performance like baseball with its – normally – 162-game season splayed out over six months. Those who try to meet that daily challenge appreciate Betts' everyday excellence even more.

"Just knowing the type of player he is – I think those are the type of players you appreciate when you see them every day," Dodgers outfielder A.J. Pollock said of Betts, who was acquired from Boston in a blockbuster trade Feb. 10, 2020.

Mookie Betts singles against the Giants on opening day for his first hit as a Dodger.
(Pasadena Star-News: Keith Birmingham)

"When you see a guy flash a 500-foot homer and they steal and they do all this stuff that's just full extension – it's just amazing. Mookie does that too. But the consistency and the focus every day, for me, I knew that's the type of player he was. I always respect those players. To me, those players are the most special because there's such a focus. It's not a flash in the pan. It's every day consistent and Mookie's done such a good job for us."

Though Betts, who signed a 12-year, $365 million contract extension with the Dodgers on July 22, has yet to hit a 500-foot home run for the Dodgers, his multi-faceted contributions have been one of the stories of the postseason.

Offensively, he has been a constant on the bases, batting .308 (16 for 52) and scoring 12 runs in 14 games. Thanks to 10 walks, Betts has a .413 on-base percentage in the postseason and has been kept off the bases just twice in those 14 games.

His baserunning has already memorably stolen two pivotal runs for the Dodgers. In Game 2 of the Division Series, the Padres had just cut the Dodgers lead to 4-3 in the seventh inning. Betts and Corey Seager were at first and second with one out when Betts initiated a double steal. Now at third base, Betts scored on a sacrifice fly and Seager on a two-out RBI single.

Without the double steal, the Dodgers score one run, maybe none. They won the game by one.

"It was just time and place in the game," Betts said. "Seags is always watching me. I told him before the season started, if I'm at second just be ready. I may make a move. I may not. But you always have to be ready."

In Game 1 of the World Series, Betts did it again. After leading off the fifth inning with a walk, Betts stole second. Perhaps distracted, Tyler Glasnow walked Seager, then watched as the Betts-Seager combo pulled off another double steal. The move sparked a four-run inning for the Dodgers in their 8-3 win.

"The pressure Mookie puts on other teams is huge for us. We've felt it before when we played him in the World Series," Dodgers catcher Austin Barnes said. "He brings a

Mookie Betts looks out over the crowd at spring training with Justin Turner and teammates. (Orange County Register: Kevin Sullivan)

different aspect to that game for us. One out with a runner on second and third is a lot different than first and second. There's a lot that can happen. I just love the way he plays."

Betts is a finalist for his fifth consecutive Gold Glove award; he won each of the past four seasons in the American League. When he wins, and it's almost a foregone conclusion, the highlight package will include three catches he has made in this postseason – coming in on Dansby Swanson's sinking line drive in Game 5 of the NLCS, going back to the wall on Marcell Ozuna's drive in Game 6 and stealing a home run from Freddie Freeman in Game 7.

In World Series Game 1, Betts became the first player in Series history to have two steals, score two runs and hit a home run in the same game. Kinda checks all the boxes and left Cody Bellinger stumped when asked if there were any more ways Betts could contribute.

"Not that I can think of. He's done just about everything. Nothing off the top of my head," Bellinger said. "He's so dedicated to doing it. Nothing's forced. He wants to do it. He wants to win and you can learn a lot from that."

With that, Bellinger reveals the other way Betts contributes. Watching a player with his talent search for every way to contribute rubs off on his teammates.

"It's really unbelievable. It's so fun to watch and we're so lucky to have him on our team," Bellinger said. "I just say – he's a superstar guy, a superstar talent. He does all the little things right. You can really learn from that when a guy's that good and wants to win and continues to do the small things that go unnoticed by a lot of people, maybe not. But it's just really special." ∎

Mookie Betts hits an RBI double against starting pitcher Brandon Woodruff of the Milwaukee Brewers during Game 2 of the National League Wild Card series. Betts' consistency at the plate and speed on the basepaths have been key elements of the Dodgers' success in 2020. (Pasadena Star-News: Keith Birmingham)

The Threads That Bind

The Rays-Dodgers World Series is Less Impersonal Than You Think

By J.P. Hoornstra • October 19, 2020

When Stuart Sternberg retired from the investment firm Goldman Sachs in 2002, he cast his eye toward buying a Major League Baseball franchise. A Brooklyn native, Sternberg was born too late to watch a Dodgers game at Ebbets Field, but he named one of his sons after his favorite pitcher, Sandy Koufax. Koufax's number 32 wound its way into his email address. Unsurprisingly, Sternberg looked into buying the Dodgers before the franchise was sold to Frank McCourt in 2004.

The Tampa Bay Devil Rays were at least Sternberg's third choice before his group purchased a large share — reportedly 48 percent — of the woebegone club in 2004. Now, 16 years later, the threads that bind the Rays and Dodgers are thick as the teams prepare for their first World Series meeting.

Those threads are often re-woven into a simple caricature. It must tie together Wall Street, and "Moneyball," and analytics, and the ruthless pursuit of efficiency in constructing a roster. It is mandatory to cite the influence of Dodgers executive Andrew Friedman, Sternberg's first hand-picked general manager in Tampa Bay and himself a Wall Street expatriate.

For all its truth, this caricature misses the mark in a critical area. It ignores the common trait most frequently mentioned by players on the two teams Monday, the Zoom-sponsored "media day" before the World Series. One man after another from both organizations picked up the thread of Rays-Dodgers connections and wove a uniquely human tale.

Rays shortstop Willy Adames summed it up best: "The way that they treat the guys, the way that they treat everybody here, makes you feel comfortable."

That's an easy thought to lose in the noise. Repeat it often enough, and it becomes hard to miss.

Consider the career trajectory of Dodgers catcher Will Smith. Two years ago, Smith was in the clubhouse for a World Series run. He didn't play an inning. He didn't make a single postseason roster. He traveled with the Dodgers in October 2018 to learn from teammates, to listen, to observe, to acclimate, months before his actual big-league debut.

"It made my transition better, getting called up last year," Smith said. "It made it a little smoother, more comfortable for myself."

Smith has never played for another organization. Neither has shortstop Corey Seager, the Most Valuable Player of the NLCS. Seager at least enjoyed some cups of coffee in spring training with the Dodgers before Friedman was hired in November 2014. How has the clubhouse culture changed since his first exposure as a teenager?

"It's become very open," Seager said. "There's nothing hidden, nothing that people are going to get upset about. We want people to feel comfortable. It's just all about showing up, doing your job, going home and moving on.

Andrew Friedman took his culture-building philosophies from Tampa Bay to Los Angeles. Rays and Dodgers players have credited that open, supportive clubhouse environment as one of the keys to success. (AP Images)

It's never nitpicking at people for how they get ready for games. It's never nitpicking on how people work. It's all about the product that night, and how do we get the best product out of everybody that night?

"We're free to figure out how people want to do it, give our advice. For the most part, we want it to be comfortable. Comfortable is a good word."

The notion of human comfort as a tenet of sabermetrics, analytics, data-driven decisions — call it what you will — is not part of the caricature. It's almost too easy to dismiss as some fancy new age mumbo jumbo. Does winning breed comfort, or does comfort breed winning? The Rays didn't enjoy a winning season in Friedman's first two years, or in 2014, his last. The Dodgers were already a winning team when Friedman replaced Ned Colletti.

Friedman might have taken his culture-building ideas from Tampa Bay to Los Angeles, but he does not take credit for their origin. They were with Sternberg from the beginning, he said, as strong as any tenet that guided the Rays' rebuild.

"So much of my growth professionally was with Stu as a mentor," Friedman said. "He has done an immeasurable amount for me and my family. And a lot of what I've learned, in a lot of respects, has come from him."

Sternberg became the Rays' managing general partner in 2005 and hasn't looked back. His influence explains why the current Rays whom Friedman did not draft, develop, or acquire echo the same thought about culture today.

"Coming over here when I got traded, I didn't know what to expect," said outfielder Austin Meadows, whom the Rays acquired from the Pirates in 2018. "How low-key everything is, how you can be yourself, that took a lot of weight off my shoulders personally. That contributed to me playing on the field, playing really well. That starts with the guys up top."

If Sternberg brought his vision for team culture from Wall Street to St. Pete, and Friedman became the public face of that vision, the man left to see it through is Rays manager Kevin Cash. Outfielder Kevin Kiermaier, the team's longest-tenured player, said Cash inherited the same approach from his predecessor, Joe Maddon.

"We've had that environment," Kiermaier said, "where it's, 'hey, show up to the field each and every day, be a professional, be yourself. Do what you need to do. As long as you handle yourself on the field each and every night, we don't care what you do, but don't cross that line or abuse what we've got going on because it's a really good thing.' Guys come over here and say that the environment, everything we do in the clubhouse behind closed doors, it's incredible to be a part of. I have to thank the players who were here before me. This is all I know. I just want to do my part … to maintain that. Little things like that go a long way for a clubhouse."

Call this World Series a triumph of data, but do not ignore its human touch. Sternberg might not have been able to save the Dodgers from the lean years of Frank McCourt, but his influence reached Chavez Ravine in its own course. That influence is too personal to be contained in a spreadsheet.

"I think there are narratives out there (about) if you use information to help guide decisions," Friedman said. "But at the core of what we do, we're involved with trying to provide the best environment and culture for people to thrive. I don't think that's different in any business. It was really important to us when I was with the Rays and it's something that is really important to us now. When guys are more comfortable, they perform better." ∎

Dodgers headwear proved to be popular items at the Official Dodger Team Store at Dodger Stadium.
(Los Angeles Daily News: Hans Gutknecht)

DODGERS.COM

ZOOK
emotion

ANC

Pasadena Star-News: Keith Birmingham

PLAYOFFS

September 30, 2020 • Los Angeles, California
Dodgers 4, Brewers 2

Off and Walking

Dodgers Edge Brewers in Game 1 with Strong Pitching Effort, Patience at the Plate

By Bill Plunkett

There was already a 14-win gap between the two teams in this Wild Card Series. When the Milwaukee Brewers lost two of their best pitchers and another starting pitcher due to injuries, they arrived for a knife fight wielding a plastic spork.

But those things can hurt.

The Dodgers scored three times in the first two innings then hung on through a series of new-age pitching machinations by both managers to take Game 1 4-2 on Wednesday night.

"The postseason is different. You don't have to have it every night," Dodgers shortstop Corey Seager said. "A walk is just as good as a hit sometimes. Like that first inning. We had three, four walks that first inning. I don't even remember what it was. You don't need to always be locked in and have to have the big hit to score runs. It's moving the lineup and getting to people and trying to score anyway you can."

Or record outs any way you can.

Clayton Kershaw and Brandon Woodruff are scheduled to start Game 2 on Thursday for the Dodgers and Brewers, respectively. That at least holds out the potential for a more turnkey pitching matchup.

Wheels were turning all game Wednesday as Dave Roberts and Craig Counsell tried to manage their way through their unique pitching challenges.

In Roberts' case, it was the blister that sent Game 1 starter Walker Buehler to the injured list twice in the last five weeks of the season. Buehler brushed off questions about his index finger Tuesday, saying everything was "fine." But it clearly remains an ongoing concern.

Before the game Wednesday, Roberts said he would be "threading the needle" on how far to push Buehler, knowing that "once you see" the blister flaring up it's too late and "understanding we need him for the next four series to win the World Series."

That thread unspooled for only four innings and 73 pitches. Buehler was dominant for the first three, allowing just one hit and striking out two an inning.

"We've talked about the cutter probably being the one (type of pitch) that's toughest on it," Buehler said. "So I mostly threw the four-seamer, the slider and the curveball tonight. It is what it is. We're managing it and moving on."

In the fourth, Buehler gave up a two-run home run to Orlando Arcia on a badly located 0-and-2 fastball. Julio Urias, moved to the bullpen in this best-of-three series, followed Buehler and contributed three scoreless innings in what look liked a pre-scripted plan but Roberts said wasn't.

"It wasn't. We just didn't know what we were going to get from Walker, to be quite honest," Roberts said. "We had a rested 'pen. I had a good idea Julio was going to pitch tonight. I just didn't know when it was going to happen. it just kind of worked more seamless which was great."

The Dodgers' offense could have made it easier for Buehler and Urias by building on the head start they were given.

Without starters Corbin Burnes (oblique) or Brett Anderson (blister), Counsell went with Brent Suter as

Dodgers starter Walker Buehler struck out eight Brewers in four innings. (Los Angeles Daily News: Hans Gutknecht)

his Game 1 starter. Suter walked just five batters in 31 2/3 innings during the regular season, but he walked four of the first seven Dodgers he faced during a 32-pitch first inning — just nine strikes.

Two Dodgers drove in runs without swinging the bat (bases-loaded walks to Will Smith and A.J. Pollock). Mookie Betts made it 3-0 with an RBI double in the second inning.

"Going into the game I don't even think he had walked a lefty all year," Seager said of Suter, who is the first pitcher in postseason history to walk in multiple runs in the first inning.

"I think we were just taking pitches we needed to, getting in good counts and then really trying to get a good pitch and not expanding the strike zone because we were ahead."

Then Counsell waved his bullpenning wand. Eric Yardley and Justin Topa retired the next 10 Dodgers in order.

Seager finally gave the Dodgers' bullpen a larger cushion, crushing a 447-foot solo home run off Freddy Peralta in the seventh. It was the 38th home run the Dodgers have hit in the seventh inning or later this year, compared to 16 allowed in those innings.

Blake Treinen pitched a scoreless eighth. But Kenley Jansen pitched an unsettling ninth. A two-out walk brought Christian Yelich to the plate as the tying run. Jansen struck him out, but Roberts sounded concerned after the game.

"It just didn't seem like the stuff had the teeth that I've seen in recent outings. I'm going to go back and look at the video," Roberts said.

"I just didn't think that the cutter — there were a couple throws that had the life, but it just didn't have the life in the zone. The breaking ball was cast more than I've seen it. We'll see. I don't know as much until I really look at it." ■

The Dodgers celebrate after defeating the Milwaukee Brewers in Game 1 of the National League Wild Card Series. (Los Angeles Daily News: Hans Gutknecht)

October 1, 2020 • Los Angeles, California
Dodgers 3, Brewers 0

Survive and Advance

Clayton Kershaw Carves Up Brewers as Dodgers Sweep Wild Card Series
By Bill Plunkett

Major League Baseball has tried to promote this year's expanded postseason field as a fall version of March Madness. If that's the case, Fairleigh Dickinson won't be advancing.

The major-league leaders in home runs this season, the Dodgers bunched three singles and a double together to break up a tense pitchers' duel with a three-run burst in the fifth inning, backing a brilliant performance by Clayton Kershaw in a 3-0 Dodgers win over the Milwaukee Brewers on Thursday night to sweep the Wild Card Series.

"This was great. This was a fun night for me. Get the postseason off to a good start," said Kershaw.

"It kind of feels like a postseason victory. Just with the expanded playoffs, it's kind of like now the postseason is starting. Nonetheless we still had to do our job. We still had to get there. Now we get to get going."

The back-to-back wins over the Brewers in the best-of-three series earned the Dodgers a four-day break before they open a best-of-five National League Division Series against the St. Louis Cardinals or San Diego Padres on Tuesday, Oct. 6.

During that time, the Dodgers will move their "bubble" to Arlington, Texas, where the rest of their postseason — however long it lasts — will play out at Globe Life Field.

"It was just a Kershaw outing. He was awesome," Dodgers catcher Austin Barnes said. "When it's clicking. it's clicking and he was clicking tonight, for sure."

It is never "just" another outing for Kershaw in October. He turned in one of the best performances of his tortured postseason life Thursday, carving up a weak Brewers lineup further limited by Ryan Braun's subtraction for Game 2.

Kershaw, who will get to pitch in his hometown for the first time in the Division Series, treated the Brewers like the .223 hitters they were during the 60-game season. He gave up three harmless singles (none after the fifth inning), walked one (then picked him off first base) and struck out a postseason career-high 13 in eight scoreless innings, matching the longest outing of his 26 postseason starts.

When the Dodgers gave him the lead, he responded by striking out the side on 12 pitches in the top of the sixth inning. Kershaw had the Brewers on their heels all night, throwing first-pitch strikes to 24 of the 27 batters he faced.

Ten of his strikeouts came with his slider as the finishing pitch and he got 33 swings and misses on the pitch out of his 93 pitches thrown.

"My last start before the season ended I really didn't feel like I had the arm speed to create the movement that I needed to on that pitch," Kershaw said. "I did a lot of kind of recovery-type things after my last start against the Angels. I think that probably helped a little bit just to get that arm speed back that you need to get that torque on that slider."

If the Brewers had a puncher's chance against the Dodgers — a major-league best 43-17 during the regular season — because of their pitching, they were down to their last knuckle in Game 2 starter Brandon Woodruff, having lost three pitchers to injuries in the days before the series.

In his 2020 playoff debut, Clayton Kershaw delivered a brilliant performance, striking out a postseason career-high 13 while allowing just three singles in eight scoreless innings. (Pasadena Star-News: Keith Birmingham)

Woodruff fired haymakers for four innings, striking out nine of the first 14 Dodgers batters. He threw eight pitches at 96 mph or higher in the first inning then mixed in more changeups and sliders as he went through the Dodgers' lineup, retiring all but one of those first 14 batters.

Finally, in the fifth inning, he was punched out. Cody Bellinger slapped a one-out single into center field and Chris Taylor followed with another single.

That brought up A.J. Pollock who bounced a ball to third baseman Luis Urias. He ran to make the force out at third base then made an off-balance throw to first. Jedd Gyorko couldn't scoop the ball out of the dirt and Pollock was safe, extending the inning.

Barnes was in the lineup because of his relationship with Kershaw. The catcher fought back from an 0-and-2 count, taking a 1-and-2 fastball off the outside edge and finally ending a six-pitch at-bat with a single to drive in the first run of the day.

"He's throwing the ball hard. I wasn't trying to do too much obviously," Barnes said. "You get too big on a guy like that he's going to miss your barrel. He threw it up and away. I was lucky to find a hole.

"Then you turn it over to Mookie. Good things happen with Mookie at the plate."

Compromised now, Woodruff fell behind Mookie Betts 2-and-0 then gave up a two-run double down the left-field line, Betts' third double in the two-game dismissal of the Brewers. As Brewers manager Craig Counsell pulled him from the game, Woodruff was ejected by home-plate umpire Quinn Wolcott, no doubt for complaining about the 1-and-2 call during Barnes' at-bat.

When the Dodgers took that 3-0 lead into the ninth inning, it was Brusdar Graterol — not Kenley Jansen — who closed it out.

"He was available," Roberts said of Jansen who he had said pregame was "absolutely" still the Dodgers closer. "He's our closer. I just felt that Brusdar, these guys hadn't seen him. Kenley is going to close out many games for us as we go forward. He understands that it's about the team and helping us win baseball games." ■

Mookie Betts doubles to drive in A.J. Pollock and Austin Barnes, breaking a scoreless tie in the fifth inning. (Pasadena Star-News: Keith Birmingham)

October 6, 2020 • Arlington, Texas
Dodgers 5, Padres 1

Slow and Steady Wins the Race

Dodgers Get a Walking Start to Beat Padres in Game 1 of NLDS

By Bill Plunkett

The zone last night … was really tight … (clap, clap, clap, clap) … deep in the heart of Texas. The Dodgers and San Diego Padres combined to draw 14 walks in Game 1 of their National League Division Series on Tuesday night at Globe Life Field, home plate umpire Lance Barrett drawing more angry glares than a Prius driver on the local highways.

The Dodgers couldn't squeeze anything out of their share of those lemons (10 in all) and didn't even have a hit through the first five innings until a four-run burst in the sixth inning sent them to a 5-1 victory over the Padres in the series opener.

The two teams combined to get just seven hits in the game (all four of the Dodgers' hits came in that sixth inning) off 14 pitchers.

"We didn't get a lot of hits early, but we took great at-bats and we made those guys work," Dodgers third baseman Justin Turner said. "We took a lot of walks tonight. When our offense is at its best, we're walking as much as we're getting hits. We did a great job of staying in the zone for the most part and getting on base."

The first five innings (which took nearly three hours to play) featured 12 walks and a hit batter but only two hits — both of them by the Padres.

Dodgers starter Walker Buehler struggled to find Barrett's strike zone, walking the bases loaded in the second inning and putting Wil Myers on that way in the fourth. Myers stole second base and scored when Buehler left an 0-and-2 fastball over the heart of the plate and Austin Nola slapped it into left field for a two-out RBI.

Buehler walked a season-high four while throwing a season-high 95 pitches, all in just four innings.

"Everything looks like a strike from the mound. It is what it is," Buehler said when asked about Barrett's strike zone. "Obviously if I look back, I'm sure a lot of those were balls that from out there I thought were strikes. But that's part of this game and I think it's a beautiful part of the game, that there's a human back there making a decision. At the end of the day, he's an umpire and his call stands. I was just trying to compete, trying to get back in the zone and that's it."

Buehler's four innings made him the longest-serving pitcher in the game.

Padres starter Mike Clevinger returned from his elbow injury and lasted just 24 pitches — 22 in a two-walk first inning and two more in the second before he left with a recurrence of that elbow issue.

The Padres used nine pitchers to shut out the St. Louis Cardinals in the decisive game of their Wild Card Series (the most pitchers used in a shutout since at least 1901) and set out to put together MLB's most crowd-sourced no-hitter.

The Dodgers had seven baserunners through the first

Mookie Betts catches a fly ball off the bat of San Diego's Tommy Pham during the ninth inning of the Dodgers' 5-1 Game 1 win. (AP Images)

four innings (six walks and a hit batter) but no hits. They scored their first run in the fifth inning without one either. Two walks, a wild pitch and a throwing error by second baseman Jake Cronenworth tied the game.

"In that situation, for myself, I just wanted to put the ball in play," said Cody Bellinger who forced the issue on Cronenworth's error by hustling down the line. "Garrett Richards has some really good stuff. Putting it in play in that situation was a win, and just bust my tail down the line and make anything happen."

Like an exhausted man juggling plates, Padres manager Jayce Tingler couldn't prevent everything from crashing down in the sixth inning.

After Chris Taylor drew a one-out — wait for it — walk, Mookie Betts tried a unique approach to reaching base. His line drive to left field went for a double, Taylor stopping at third. A sacrifice fly scored Taylor. Justin Turner followed with an RBI single and Max Muncy doubled off the wall in left-center. An infield single and a wild pitch pushed across two more runs.

The Padres went through three pitchers in that inning alone (on their way to using nine in a game for the third time in four postseason games). The frequent trips to the mound became a strain on the Tingler-Barrett relationship and Barrett ejected the Padres manager from the game before he could get back to the dugout following one pitching change.

"He said he warned me three times (for arguing balls and strikes before the ejection)," Tingler said. "I can't hear. You can't hear. I like Lance. Lance is good. But we disagreed on the strike zone. Simple as that."

Tingler's mood likely did not improve, watching from the clubhouse as the Dodgers' bullpen slammed the door shut. Dustin May, Victor Gonzalez, Blake Treinen and Kenley Jansen followed Buehler with five scoreless innings, allowing just one baserunner — a leadoff double by Trent Grisham in the eighth.

And no walks.

"It's hard to fathom what Dustin May, Victor, Treinen and then Kenley did to come out and shut them down like that," Buehler said. "It's a testament to what we do here. I've got a lot of pride to be a part of this." ■

Walker Buehler walked four and threw 95 pitches in four innings, but struck out eight and allowed just one run. (AP Images)

October 7, 2020 • Arlington, Texas
Dodgers 6, Padres 5

In MVP Form

Cody Bellinger Saves the Day as Dodgers Take Game 2 Against Padres
By Bill Plunkett

For one night, Cody Bellinger was the most valuable player again.

Bellinger jumped at the wall in center field and reached over it to rob Fernando Tatis Jr. of a two-run home run that would have flipped the score and erased a Dodgers lead in the seventh inning. The spectacular catch prompted Dodgers pitcher Brusdar Graterol — who served up the blast to Tatis — to shed his hat and glove in celebration near the mound.

Bellinger held on to Tatis' drive more securely than the Dodgers held on to that lead. They had to survive another shaky ninth inning by Kenley Jansen — likely his last this October — before they could beat the Padres, 6-5, in Game 2 of their National League Division Series on Wednesday night.

"Great players make great plays in big moments and Cody did just that," Dodgers manager Dave Roberts said. "I just don't know many guys that can make that play. … His length and his ability to jump and control his body. It was a game-changing play."

It was potentially a series-changing play. Since losing to the Padres at Petco Park on Sept. 14, the Dodgers have won 14 of 16 games and have now pushed the Padres to the brink of elimination in this best-of-five NLDS.

"It's going to take me a while to wind down from that one," Bellinger said upon entering the post-game interview room. "That's postseason baseball right there."

Settling in for what could be a long residency at Globe Life Field, the Dodgers sprayed nine hits — including one (gasp) home run — around the expansive field while building a 4-1 lead through five innings against Padres starter Zach Davies.

Corey Seager found the gaps for a pair of doubles, driving in two runs in the third inning then scoring on a two-out RBI single by Max Muncy. Bellinger launched a 433-foot solo home run off the hitting backdrop beyond the center field wall — measuring the distance for his eventual heroics.

"I knew I hit that ball well, but I haven't hit a ball (out) to center field in batting practice, I don't think," said Bellinger, whose homer was the first in this series by either team. "So I was, 'Damn, I hope that goes.' It was nice to see it hit the wall — over the wall.

"I was, 'Damn, I got some juice.' That's what I thought."

The lead should have made Kershaw comfortable, but he was not as dominant as he was during the Wild Card Series — not surprising given the greater degree of difficulty facing the Padres instead of the Milwaukee Brewers.

Kershaw gave up an RBI double to Wil Myers in the second inning — after holding Myers to a 5-for-40 line, five singles and 14 strikeouts in their previous meetings — and stranded runners at the corners in the fourth.

Trouble found him in the sixth inning when Manny Machado lined a 2-and-1 slider over the left field wall to

Cody Bellinger leaps to rob San Diego's Fernando Tatis Jr. of a home run in the seventh inning of Game 2. (AP Images)

lead off the inning. The ball left Machado's bat at 108 mph. No exit velocity was available for the bat as Machado chucked it toward the Padres dugout, screaming, "Let's (expletive) go" in a moment reminiscent of Trent Grisham's posturing after a solo home run off Kershaw in San Diego last month.

The exhortation seemed to work when Eric Hosmer made it back-to-back home runs. It was a one-run game, 4-3, and the vuvuzela in the Padres' family section came back to life.

"My last start of the regular season was pretty bad. Against the Brewers (in the Wild Card Series), I felt like I had a lot of stuff going," Kershaw said. "This one was kind of right in the middle of those two. I wish there was a magic formula to have everything going the way you want it to every game. But sometimes it doesn't work that way."

Kershaw avoided the inning that has been the dark alley of many of his postseason nightmares. Blake Treinen handled the first two outs of the seventh inning, but he hit Grisham with a pitch and Roberts brought in Graterol to face Tatis.

Tatis turned on Graterol's first pitch, a 99-mph fastball on the outer half, and drove it 407 feet to straightaway center field. Bellinger chased it and met it at the wall, timing his jump expertly and reaching over to make the catch.

"I knew he hit it. So in my head it was either, 'Alright, that's gone off the black screen or I'm going to get to the wall and maybe have a chance to catch it,'" Bellinger said. "Just turned around as fast as I could, got to the fence and saw that it was rob-able and tried to time up my jump."

Near the mound, Graterol flung his hat and glove away in celebration, drawing the disapproval of Machado — apparently untroubled by irony — when Graterol blew kisses toward the Padres dugout.

The display set off both dugouts with Machado loudly repeating an obscenity aimed at the Dodgers and several Dodgers waving him away.

"When he hit his home run, he threw the bat away, this, that and the other," Dodgers outfielder Mookie Betts said on Fox's post-game. "When we take one away, we can celebrate too. It's got to be two sides to it."

Betts did his part, leading a double steal that helped the Dodgers add two insurance runs in the bottom of the seventh. They needed them.

Graterol retired the Padres (including Machado) in order in the eighth and Roberts handed the three-run lead to Jansen. It was a move he came to regret.

After an infield single off Jansen (literally), Mitch Moreland drove an RBI double into the right-center field gap, bringing the tying run to the plate. Jansen got Austin Nola to pop out, but Grisham singled Moreland home and Roberts had to go get Jansen.

The Dodgers' all-time saves leader, Jansen might not be trusted in another ninth inning this postseason.

"I'm going to keep thinking through it," Roberts said. "There were some good throws in there and there was a dropped third strike to Grisham and he ended up getting a base hit. I'm going to think through it. It was just a lot for him — 30 pitches to get two outs. I know that he's disappointed as well. But I'll keep thinking through it."

Joe Kelly came in and added to the tension, walking Tatis and Machado to load the bases before getting Hosmer to ground out to end the game.

"Never a doubt, never a doubt," Kershaw joked afterward. "That's how Joe Kelly rolls. He likes to make it interesting for us." ■

Joe Kelly came on in relief of Kenley Jansen in the ninth inning to end a Padres rally and earn the save. (AP Images)

October 8, 2020 • Arlington, Texas
Dodgers 12, Padres 3

Been There, Done That

Dodgers Take Care of Business, Complete NLDS Sweep of Padres

By Bill Plunkett

Family members (quarantining with their respective teams) were invited to attend the National League Division Series games at Globe Life Field this week, set up in special seating areas at field level just past the dugouts.

The San Diego Padres' family area was the more raucous. They brought Thundersticks to Game 1 and at least one vuvuzela to Game 2.

The Dodgers' family section, by contrast, exuded more of a "been there, done that" vibe for most of the series.

Their significant others on the field for the Dodgers treated it like a business trip, taking care of theirs by collecting 14 hits — including a postseason record-tying five by Will Smith — in a 12-3 dismissal of the Padres on Thursday night, sweeping their best-of-five NLDS.

T-shirts and hats were passed out and a team photo was taken on the field. But the celebration was once again fairly tame — as it was after the division-clinching victory and last week's Wild Card Series sweep.

"We did our job today. Move on to the next round," Dodgers outfielder A.J. Pollock said. "We're all excited. We're happy. We're going to celebrate together. But we did what we wanted to do. We did what we were supposed to do. Obviously, we're going to celebrate that. But we expected it."

The Dodgers will face the Atlanta Braves in the best-of-seven NL Championship Series beginning Monday (still at Globe Life Field). It is the Dodgers' fifth trip to the NLCS in the past eight seasons — the Braves' first since 2001. But both arrive undefeated in the postseason, the Dodgers having outscored the Milwaukee Brewers and Padres 30-11 in their five wins. The Braves beat the Cincinnati Reds and

Miami Marlins by a total score of 24-5, pitching shutouts in four of their five games (the first time a team has done that to start the postseason since 1905).

"Everyone's gone above and beyond," Dodgers manager Dave Roberts said of a team that has dominated during baseball's pandemic season. "This is a unique year. It's sort of, in a unique way, galvanized us. We have a lot of work still to do. But I'm really proud of everyone."

The Padres faced the Dodgers with two arms tied behind their backs — injured starters Dinelson Lamet and Mike Clevinger (who lasted just two innings in Game 1). Bullpen games were a way of life for them during their brief postseason visit. They used nine pitchers to shut out the St. Louis Cardinals in the deciding game of their Wild Card Series.

They used 11 (an MLB record for any postseason game) with far less success Thursday.

What the Padres did out of desperation, the Dodgers did out of design Thursday.

With five starting pitchers to choose from — two who hadn't even pitched in the series yet (Julio Urias and Tony Gonsolin) — they gave the ball to Dustin May for Game 3. Then they took it away after just three batters and 16 pitches (five of which registered 100 or 101 mph). Adam Kolarek came in for the second inning, aimed at a left-handed stretch of the Padres' lineup.

"It was kind of read-and-react," Roberts said of using May as an opener after using him for two innings in relief in Game 1. "I just felt that Dustin had one, two innings, maybe three at the most. I felt like there was a good run after that for Kolarek and then having Julio (Urias) behind him it just kind of went that way. There was nothing really

Mookie Betts scored three of the Dodgers' 12 runs in Game 3. (AP Images)

scripted like that. We just had guys lined up and good lanes for them."

The strategy looked like another instance of the Dodgers' sophisticated front office overthinking a pitching strategy in October, getting in their own way, when the Padres scored twice off Kolarek — albeit with soft contact and a pair of walks — in the second inning to take an early lead.

The merits of the strategy got stronger when Urias came in and struck out Fernando Tatis Jr. with the bases loaded. It got stronger when the Dodgers sent nine batters to the plate in the third inning and scored five times. It looked positively brilliant when Urias retired the first 10 batters he faced.

"You could talk about the play of the game was the first hitter that he faced," Roberts said. "It was a bases-loaded situation. He punches Tatis. That could have been a different game. Right there, that just flipped the game."

It was Urias' second appearance as a "bulk" innings reliever in this postseason and he has allowed just one unearned run and four hits over eight innings — the equivalent of one outstanding start, spread out over two games like a sandwich maker running out of mustard.

By the time Urias gave up his only hit to the Padres, it was the sixth inning and the Dodgers had collected 11 hits of their own while building an 8-2 lead.

Smith had three singles and two doubles in the game, driving in three runs. It was only the ninth five-hit game in postseason history, the first since Albert Pujols had five hits (including three home runs) in Game 3 of the 2011 World Series across the street at the abandoned Ballpark in Arlington.

"I go one at-bat at a time," said Smith, who started the postseason 0 for 11 despite some solid contact. "As long as I'm finding good quality at-bats, good quality contact I'm happy. I never really got down on myself for not having any hits. Each new at-bat I could help the team win. But, yeah, it was nice to get some hits tonight."

Cody Bellinger had two hits and three RBIs, including two on a triple. Pollock had two hits, drove in a run and scored twice. Mookie Betts was on base three times (a double and two walks) and scored each time. Justin Turner drove in a run with a single, his 64th postseason hit (a Dodgers franchise record).

"Records are cool," Turner said. "Championships are better." ∎

The Dodgers pose for a team photo after completing their NLDS sweep of the San Diego Padres to advance to the NLCS for the fourth time in the last five seasons. (AP Images)

National League Championship Series Game 1

October 12, 2020 • Arlington, Texas
Braves 5, Dodgers 1

Opening Thud

Braves Erupt in Ninth Inning, Beat Dodgers in Game 1

By Bill Plunkett

Whatever issues the Dodgers might have with the ninth inning this postseason, they are apparently not limited to Kenley Jansen.

Austin Riley made a mockery of Globe Life Field's spacious dimensions, launching a sinker that didn't sink enough from Dodgers reliever Blake Treinen 448 feet into the seats in left-center field to start the ninth inning and break a tie. Three more runs followed, and the Atlanta Braves beat the Dodgers 5-1 in Game 1 of the National League Championship Series on Monday night.

"(Max) Fried threw the ball really well. And then they have a really good bullpen just like we do," said Kiké Hernandez, who hit a home run in the fifth inning off Fried for the Dodgers' only run. "At the end of the day, we came up short because we didn't put at-bats together. We didn't get runners on base. We weren't able to pass the baton like we did in the last series."

The Braves' pitching staff came into the NLCS off a historic start to the postseason. No team since the 1905 New York Giants had started the postseason with four shutouts in the first five games.

There was reason to give that performance the side-eye, however. The Braves' shutouts had come against the Cincinnati Reds and Miami Marlins — playoff teams in name only and two lower-tier offenses during the mini-season. The Dodgers posed a much bigger challenge.

Game 1 starter Max Fried gave all those zeroes legitimacy.

The Dodgers put runners on first and second with two outs in the first and second innings, using the same single-walk combination. But Fried escaped damage and retired seven consecutive batters following the second walk.

The Harvard-Westlake product struck out nine

and, like Dodgers starter Walker Buehler, made just one mistake. His was a hanging 0-and-2 curveball to Hernandez in the fifth inning. Hernandez deposited it over the wall in left field for a solo home run.

"They made some mistakes that we just didn't capitalize on," Dodgers manager Dave Roberts said. "But you could see that their plan was just to spin us a lot more.

"I thought the first two innings we did a really nice job (driving up Fried's pitch count). Then the second time through we got a little bit out of our game. To his credit, he just kept nibbling and spinning us to death and got through six."

Buehler matched Fried but he did not make it look easy. He served up a solo home run in the first inning to Freddie Freeman — a 111-mph drive crushed 429 feet into the right field seats, freshly occupied by live fans. And he had to navigate around runners in scoring position in each of the next three innings.

A career-high five walks and seven strikeouts along the way pushed his pitch count to a season-high 100 after back-to-back singles to start the sixth. Brusdar Graterol defused that situation.

Dustin May followed Graterol and gave up a double to Marcell Ozuna to start the eighth inning. An intentional walk and the gentlest of hit-by-pitches loaded the bases with two outs.

Victor Gonzalez ended that threat, striking out pinch-hitter Charlie Culberson.

In both cases, Graterol (three outs on six pitches) and Gonzalez (four pitches) expended little but Roberts did not ask them to come out for the next inning.

"With Brusdar he took a ball, that last one off the palm of his hand," Roberts said of a comebacker that ended the sixth. "I just felt that was it right there. I

Freddie Freeman crosses the plate after hitting a home run in the first inning of Game 1 to give the Braves an early 1-0 lead. (AP Images)

expect him to be ready to go tomorrow. And with Victor, punching out (pinch-hitter Charlie) Culberson but … I really loved Blake taking down that inning."

His love was misplaced — just like the 1-and-2 fastball Treinen left over the heart of the plate to Riley. The 23-year-old crushed it and said he "didn't feel my legs when I was running the bases."

"I was able to hit a home run when I debuted (in May 2019)," Riley said. "This one tops it by far. The game is on the line, postseason, put the team ahead — that's what it's all about."

Treinen's night didn't get better. Ronald Acuña Jr. followed with a double. After a fly out moved him to third, Ozuna drove him in with a single.

"I just felt that run right there (in the Braves' lineup) was really good for Blake," Roberts said. "He's going to

have to do it again. It just didn't work out. I just trust that he's going to get those guys out."

Treinen got just one of the four batters he faced. Jake McGee replaced him and gave up a deep fly to Ozzie Albies that was caught … by Braves closer Mark Melancon warming up in the bullpen, showing that the Braves' bullpen can do it all. Chris Martin, Will Smith and Melancon followed Fried by retiring the final nine Dodgers batters in order, closing out a four-hitter.

"It's baseball. It's going to happen. We're going to lose games," Hernandez said of the Dodgers' first defeat in nearly three weeks (since Sept. 23). "But you know what? Game 1 doesn't mean anything if they don't win four games this series. Whoever wins four games first is the one that wins the series. We'll throw this one away and come back tomorrow with a fresh mind and do what we do." ∎

National League Championship Series Game 2

October 13, 2020 • Arlington, Texas
Braves 8, Dodgers 7

Coming Up Short

Dodgers' Offense Arrives Late but Braves Take 2-0 NLCS Lead

By Bill Plunkett

It was too little. It might not be too late.

Down by seven runs after six innings on Tuesday night at Globe Life Field, the Dodgers looked like they would become the Atlanta Braves' fifth shutout victim in seven postseason games.

The Dodgers avoided that fate with a seventh-inning three-run home run by Corey Seager and then fought back within a run, getting the tying run to third base in the ninth inning before losing 8-7 to the Braves in Game 2 of the National League Championship Series.

By scoring seven runs in the final three innings, the kings of the late innings during the regular season gave themselves a pulse heading into Game 3.

"This team has a lot of fight. We've done it all year," said Seager, who drove in the Dodgers' first four runs in Game 2. "We were one swing, one anything away from tying that ballgame and going into extras. It's never over 'til it's over. This is a long series and we're up to the challenge."

They will have to buck history. Since the LCS went to a best-of-seven format in 1985, teams in the AL and NL that have taken 2-0 leads have gone on to win 28 of 31 times.

In the Dodgers' own recent history, this is the third time during their current run of eight consecutive postseason appearances that they have lost the first two games of a series. The other two — the 2018 World Series against the Boston Red Sox and 2013 NLCS against the St. Louis Cardinals — each ended badly for the Dodgers.

"It's just one game at a time," Dodgers manager Dave Roberts said. "I know it's a cliché but that's the only way to do it and the only way to approach it. I thought just late, us showing some life offensively was good to see.

"To see us fighting, that was a good thing."

Freddie Freeman is likely to collect the National League MVP award for the 2020 season next month. He hit a home run for the second consecutive game and drove in three runs as the Braves built their big lead. The two MVP winners in the Dodgers' lineup — Mookie Betts (the American League MVP in 2018) and Cody Bellinger (the NL MVP last season) — were a combined 0 for 13 in this series before rousing from their slumber during a three-run ninth.

They aren't alone in taking the collar against Braves pitching. As a team, the Dodgers have hit .209 (14 for 67) — with four of those hits coming in the ninth inning of Game 2.

The Dodgers wasted early opportunities that loomed larger only after the 4-hour, 12-minute game reached its final moments. They drew five walks in the first four innings, had runners at first and second with two outs in the first inning and the bases loaded in the third.

Nothing came of any of it, thanks in part to an outstanding play by Braves third baseman Austin Riley on Will Smith's bullet in the first inning. Nothing came of Chris Taylor's 400-foot drive to center field, 103 mph off the bat, to lead off the third inning either. Ronald Acuña Jr. flagged it down at the wall.

"It's just been a battle for us the past two days," Seager said. "They've thrown some good games and we just have to make the adjustments."

The Dodgers had to content themselves with working rookie starter Ian Anderson's pitch count up high enough (85) to get into the Braves' bullpen early.

Ozzie Albies beats the throw for a two-out single in the seventh inning of Game 2. (AP Images)

The Dodgers had to wait for their reward in Game 2. They were down 7-0 by the time Seager struck his three-run shot off Braves lefty A.J. Minter. His double drove in Betts with another run in the ninth. Max Muncy followed with a two-run home run and Smith reached on an error.

The Dodgers' rally was built against some relievers they would not have seen in a closer game — Darren O'Day, A.J. Minter and Josh Tomlin were charged with six of the Dodgers' seven runs. But when Bellinger tripled into the right field corner with two outs in the ninth, Braves closer Mark Melancon was in the game. Smith scored and the tying run was stunningly just 90 feet from scoring. A.J. Pollock grounded out to end the game.

Tabbed to start Game 2 when Clayton Kershaw had to be scratched due to back spasms, Tony Gonsolin was perfect through the first three innings — and very imperfect after that. Just as he had against Walker Buehler in the first inning of Game 1, Freeman took an inside fastball and rifled it into the right field seats.

The two-run home run put the Braves on top to stay. They have scored first in each of their seven games this postseason. But they weren't done.

The Braves scored four times in the fifth inning, chasing Gonsolin from the game and piling on against Pedro Baez. Gonsolin and Baez tied an LCS record by issuing four walks in the inning (including one by Baez with the bases loaded). Freeman ripped an RBI single off Baez after Roberts brought the right-handed Baez in to face him.

Roberts had Blake Treinen warming up at one point as Gonsolin faded. Adam Kolarek would have come in to face Freeman in the days before the three-batter minimum rule. So Roberts went with Baez and the Braves pounced.

"You're in a tough spot with that three-batter rule," Roberts said. "It's 3-0 there. To think about bringing in one of your highest-leverage relievers (like Treinen or Brusdar Graterol) in the fifth inning of a three-run deficit game just doesn't make sense there.

"You just can't play every game, regardless of score, like it's life or death in a seven-game series."

The Braves added a run off Alex Wood in the seventh and then capped the night with their new postseason tradition — a home run by Ozzie Albies caught by Melancon in the Braves' bullpen. That proved to be the deciding run. ∎

Atlanta's Nick Markakis scores past the tag of catcher Will Smith to give the Braves a 3-0 lead in the fifth inning. (AP Images)

October 14, 2020 • Arlington, Texas
Dodgers 15, Braves 3

Riding the Wave

Dodgers Set Records with 11-Run First Inning in Game 3 Demolition of Braves
By Bill Plunkett

The Dodgers showed life with a late rally in Game 2.

In Game 3, they dialed it up to … 11.

The road team for the first time in this neutral-site National League Championship Series, the Dodgers batted first in Game 3 and made history before the Atlanta Braves could even get back in the dugout.

The top of the first inning lasted 32 minutes and featured 14 batters who collected seven hits, including three home runs and two doubles, walked three times and scored 11 runs. Ten of the runs came after Braves starter Kyle Wright had recorded two outs — the only outs he would get.

The Dodgers set postseason records for runs and total bases (18) in a single inning and tied the postseason record for home runs (three) and extra-base hits (five) in an inning.

And by rule, they got to bat again.

When the damage was done, the Dodgers had pounded their way back into this best-of-seven series with a 15-3 demolition of the Braves on Wednesday night, tying the record for runs, extra-base hits and total bases in an NLCS game.

The game lasted 4 hours and 15 minutes, one-minute short of matching the longest nine-inning game in NLCS history. But only those first 32 minutes mattered.

"I'd say it was a pretty light attitude (before the game). A lot of guys were joking around," Max Muncy said of the team's mood. "And that doesn't surprise me at all. We know who we are over here. We're a really good team. We kind of lost our footing those first two games. But like I said, we all know who we are. We weren't worried about anything and tonight we went out and showed what we can do."

Suddenly a bandbox, cavernous Globe Life Field yielded six home runs — one to each of the five left-handed hitters in the Dodgers' starting lineup (Muncy, Joc Pederson, Edwin Rios, Corey Seager and Cody Bellinger) plus one to Braves center fielder Cristian Pache.

Pederson and Rios went deep back-to-back in the historic first inning, producing four runs between them. Then Muncy matched that with one swing, capping the 11-run explosion with a grand slam.

"That was fun to be a part of," said Pederson, who finished the night with four hits. "I think some of the momentum from last night, that last inning, definitely carried over and got us feeling a lot more comfortable at the plate. It was fun to be a part of."

It started with the tiniest of advantages.

Mookie Betts led off with a ground ball to third base and was called out at first when the throw stretched Freddie Freeman. The Dodgers challenged the call and it was overturned. Seager ripped a double into the left-center field gap on the next pitch and the Dodgers were the first team to score before the Braves in any of their eight postseason games this year.

Max Muncy celebrates after hitting a grand slam in the first inning. Muncy's blast capped an 11-run first-inning explosion by the Dodgers. (AP Images)

"It was obviously a really, really, really close play and it turned in our favor," Pederson said of Betts' infield single to start the game. "For some reason, that just got the whole bench … excited and we just ran with that momentum."

Bellinger led off the second with his home run and Seager went deep in the third inning. In his last two at-bats in Game 2, Seager drove in four runs with a homer and a double. In his first three at-bats in Game 3, he drove in three more with a double, single and homer.

By the time Pache led off the bottom of the third with his first major-league home run and the Braves' first hit of the game, the Dodgers had scored all 15 of their runs.

After the Dodgers rallied late in Game 2, Betts said it "absolutely" could provide momentum even if the Dodgers were down 0-2 in the best-of-seven series. His advice before Game 3 was to "just stay on that wave."

It was a big breaker.

In the first 15 innings of this series, Braves pitching held the Dodgers to a .120 batting average (.120), one extra-base hit (Kiké Hernandez's Game 1 homer) and one run (same) while striking out 17 batters.

In the next six innings (the last three of Game 2, the first three of Game 3), the Dodgers hit .525 (21 for 40) with 12 extra-base hits (seven homers, four doubles, one triple) and scored 22 runs.

Wright lasted just nine batters, retired only two, and the Dodgers laid waste to reliever Grant Dayton as well.

Faced with the prospect of bullpen games on each of the next two days — rookie right-hander Bryse Wilson will start the parade in Game 4 — the Braves did what they could to save their bullets after that, rolling out right-hander Huascar Ynoa to soak up four scoreless innings and serve as the Braves' hero of the night.

"Quite honestly, we're in better shape than if we'd grinded out a 7-5 loss," Braves manager Brian Snitker said of Ynoa's bullpen-saving performance. "If we had to lose a game, that's probably the best possible way."

Handed a double-digit lead before he touched the mound, Julio Urias went the first five innings for the Dodgers, throwing a career-high 101 pitches. With the potential for four games ahead in this series, Dodgers manager Dave Roberts said there was no thought given to pulling Urias after the big early lead and making him an option in those other games.

"No. I think getting some other guys not pitching was important as well," Roberts said. "He'll have a couple days off and we'll see where he's at then.

"I don't think right now we're worried about Game 7."

Roberts did find a soft spot for struggling closer Kenley Jansen to get some work, sending him out for the sixth inning.

It was the earliest Jansen had entered a game since Game 6 of the 2016 NLCS when he pitched the sixth through eighth innings as the Chicago Cubs closed out the Dodgers. Jansen retired the Braves in order (though Bellinger had to go to the wall in center field for one fly ball). ∎

Cody Bellinger homers leading off the second inning to extend the Dodgers lead to 12-0. (AP Images)

October 15, 2020 • Arlington, Texas
Braves 10, Dodgers 2

On the Canvas

Dodgers on Brink of Elimination After Another Braves Rookie Stifles Them in NLCS
By Bill Plunkett

After losing the first two games of the National League Championship Series, the Dodgers didn't think it was time to worry. "We all know who we are," Max Muncy said.

Looking at three consecutive pitching matchups that seemed to tilt heavily in their favor, the Dodgers weren't worried. "Just win a game and stay on that wave," Mookie Betts said.

After exploding for a record-setting 11 runs in the first inning of Game 3, it certainly wasn't time to worry.

But now — it's time to worry. After losing 10-2 to the Atlanta Braves in Game 4 on Thursday night, the Dodgers have been pushed to the brink of elimination from another postseason that was supposed to validate their regular-season excellence.

Braves DH Marcell Ozuna outhit the Dodgers, 4-3. You don't win many postseason games when an opposing player outhits your entire lineup.

"You know what — they still have to beat us another time. I still believe in every single guy in that clubhouse," Dodgers manager Dave Roberts said after another postseason press conference spent fending off questions about his bullpen usage and defending an offense that came up short again.

Facing the Atlanta Braves' third rookie starter in four games, the Dodgers managed just one hit in the first six innings. Bryse Wilson was playing baseball and football at Orange High School in Hillsborough, North Carolina when Clayton Kershaw was winning Cy Young awards.

But he outpitched the future Hall of Famer for six innings Thursday night, staying longer than the Braves could have hoped in their most optimistic dreams, while Kershaw's legacy was once again kicked in the teeth by his postseason narrative when the Braves exploded for six runs in the sixth inning.

"They're similar to us as far as they build on momentum really well," Kershaw said of that sixth inning. "It seems like they have that domino effect when one thing gets going. They just continue to build on that. They've got good hitters too. They're a good team. We just have to come back and win tomorrow."

Rookies have pitched 14-2/3 innings for the Braves in this series. Take away the disastrous two-thirds that Kyle Wright suffered through in Game 3 and those novices have held 2020's most productive offense to one run and three hits in 14 innings.

Wilson spent most of this summer at the Braves' alternate training site and had just seven big-league starts scattered over the past three seasons to his credit before Game 4 with a 5.91 career ERA.

But he retired 18 of the 20 Dodgers hitters he faced, allowing one walk and Rios' solo home run, driven into the swirling winds of Globe Life Field on a cool night when Texas' most expensive box canyon could have used a roof. Oh, wait — it has one, but MLB elected to keep it open despite the blustery conditions, having committed to this course when it allowed fans in the park during the coronavirus pandemic.

"At the end of the day, yes, it's the postseason. Yes, it's the championship series, crucial game," Wilson said. "But for me, it's just baseball. It's me throwing to the catcher, getting hitters out."

Oh — if it could only be that simple for Kershaw in October.

Pitching on seven days' rest after back spasms postponed his first start in this NLCS, Kershaw had baserunners in four of the first five innings. But his only mistake was a low slider that Ozuna drove into the wind and off the facing of the second deck in left field.

Tied at 1-1, it all came crashing down on Kershaw in

Ronald Acuna Jr. beats the throw for a single to lead off the sixth inning of Game 2. Acuna later scored the go-ahead run on a Freddie Freeman double. (AP Images)

the sixth — as it has too many times in past Octobers.

Ronald Acuña Jr. beat out an infield single to start the inning and went to second when Kiké Hernandez's attempt at a highlight-reel play bounced past Muncy and into the photo well. Freddie Freeman bounced a double into the right field corner for his fifth RBI of the series.

"It would have been nice to get Acuña out. He's pretty quick right there," Kershaw said. "It's just part of playing on turf. He chopped one in there. Freddie, I had two strikes on him. Probably went one too many pitches inside. He hit it good, but it was on the ground. Still with two strikes, probably gotta make a better pitch.

"That's a tough way to go for that sixth inning, for sure."

As Brusdar Graterol watched from the Dodgers' bullpen, Kershaw faced Ozuna for the third time in the game having been hit hard in each of the two previous at-bats (a double play and the first of his two home runs).

The NL leader in home runs and RBIs this season laced an RBI double into the left-center gap and Kershaw exited the postseason stage, head down and shoulders slumped again.

"The inning prior was a clean inning. He punched

the last guy," Roberts said. "You induce weak contact, tough play and it gets away from the first baseman and he gets second base. There's another ground ball by the first baseman. We had Freeman played way over in the gap and it turns a single into a double.

"I'm not going to take Clayton out after a weak ground ball and another ground ball off the bat of Freeman. … I felt really good with Clayton at that time."

Graterol and Victor Gonzalez couldn't stop the bleeding. They gave up a series of well-placed hits including a two-run double by Dansby Swanson, shot past a diving Justin Turner, and RBI singles by Austin Riley and Cristian Pache.

The Dodgers mounted a response in the seventh inning, pushing across a run and loading the bases for Will Smith with two outs. Facing the defense that shifted less than any other team during the regular season, Smith hit a line drive through the middle — and into the glove of Ozzie Albies, shifted behind second base.

Ozuna fought the wind and won again in the bottom of the seventh, his second home run of the night leaving the Dodgers on the canvas. ■

October 16, 2020 • Arlington, Texas
Dodgers 7, Braves 3

Big Willie Style

Dodgers Extend NLCS with Home Runs from Will Smith, Corey Seager
By Bill Plunkett

Will Smith couldn't lose.

In a moment straight out of a Hollywood script — namely "Gemini Man" — young Dodgers catcher Will Smith came to the plate in the sixth inning on Friday night with the Dodgers trailing by a run and Atlanta Braves lefty reliever Will Smith on the mound.

It was a moment big enough for two Will Smiths and Will Smith got the better of it, launching a three-run home run into the left-field seats and giving the Dodgers the lead. With Corey Seager — the one and only, as far as we know — hitting two home runs, the Dodgers beat the Braves, 7-3, in Game 5 of the National League Championship Series.

The win allows the Dodgers to continue "The Pursuit of Happyness," extending the NLCS to a Game 6.

"Will doing what he did was awesome," Seager said. "That's the big moment but you need the big hit and he got it."

For the first five innings, the Dodgers were in desperate need of a leading man.

Save for a six-inning burst in mid-series (the last three innings of Game 2 and the first three of Game 3), the Dodgers were being dominated by an assortment of Braves pitchers. The Game 5 starter, lefty A.J. Minter, was expected to "open" a bullpen game for the starter-depleted Braves in Game 5. In his first start since college (Texas A&M), Minter hogged the spotlight. He retired nine of the 10 Dodgers batters he faced in three innings, striking out seven of them.

Before the game, Dodgers manager Dave Roberts said he was hoping for "a Walker Buehler moment" from his starter Dustin May, referring to Buehler's outstanding start as a rookie in Game 163 two years ago. May wasn't up to that moment. (Buehler will get his chance at another one in Game 6.)

May lasted just two innings, fighting his way through heavy underbrush but giving up just a run in each inning. The Braves were in danger of breaking the game open in the third against Joe Kelly, though. Back-to-back singles were followed by a ground out to put runners at second and third for Dansby Swanson.

Swanson hit a sinking liner to right field that Mookie Betts charged, catching it at his shoe tops.

"It's definitely a tough play," Betts said. "A lot of it is instinctual. I just knew I needed to stay on my feet in order to get a throw off and have a chance at him at home. So my whole plan was to do whatever I can to stay on my feet."

Betts' throw home was too late to beat Marcell Ozuna, who had tagged up at third base.

Or not.

The Dodgers challenged the call and replay showed Ozuna drifting down the third-base line as Betts made the catch. Instead of a lead-expanding sacrifice fly for the Braves, the Dodgers had an inning-ending double play.

"That was a huge momentum twist for us," Seager said. "It's not always on the offensive side that you get a spark. A big play like that in a big moment, that changes everything for you."

Dodgers catcher Will Smith homers off of Braves reliever Will Smith to give the Dodgers the lead in the sixth inning. (AP Images)

The Dodgers' record 11-run first inning in Game 3 was sparked by an overturned call — allowing Betts to beat out a game-starting infield single. This one lit a slow-burning fuse.

Seager led off the fourth inning with a solo home run (one of his four in the series) but it wasn't until the sixth that the Dodgers' offense fully awakened.

Betts beat out another infield single to start it (no need for replay on this one). A two-out walk by Max Muncy put two runners on brought on the worlds-colliding matchup of Will Smiths.

"I mean, it's a common enough name," the Dodgers' Will Smith said, admitting he knows at least three other Will Smiths — the famous one, another one he went to high school with and the one he faced at Globe Life Field.

"I'll always bet on our Will Smith," Roberts said.

One got ahead of the other, 0-and-2, but the younger Smith stayed disciplined, working the count full and then collecting his reward — a fastball down and in that he turned on.

"I was just trying to kind of push him out over (the plate), get a good pitch to hit, not let him bully me in there," Smith said. "He made a mistake. I capitalized on it."

The lead got bigger in the seventh when another replay overturn went the Dodgers' way. Home plate umpire Dan Iassogna ruled Chris Taylor was hit by a pitch. The Braves challenged that one and it showed the pitch had hit Taylor's bat.

So Taylor went back to the plate, doubled to left and scored on a single by Betts, all with two outs. Seager hit the next pitch for his second home run of the game and the margin for error in Roberts' decision-making got a whole lot larger.

He had nine outs to get from a bullpen that allowed 15 runs in 15-2/3 innings over the first four games of this NLCS. The Braves got one more, but the Dodgers closed it out the old-fashioned way — with Kenley Jansen recording the last three outs, all via strikeout.

"It's win or go home. It's simple," Seager said of the Dodgers' immediate future. "There's no extra pressure. It is what it is. We know what's at stake. Every game in any series, it's winning that day. It's not looking forward. It's not looking to the next day. It's about tomorrow and winning." ∎

The Dodgers dugout erupts after catcher Will Smith's sixth-inning home run to give the Dodgers the lead. (AP Images)

October 17, 2020 • Arlington, Texas
Dodgers 3, Braves 1

Back from the Brink

Dodgers Strike Early, Hold on to Force Game 7 in NLCS
By Bill Plunkett

Apparently, it's not over until they say it is. Others said it was after the Dodgers lost the first two games of this National League Championship Series or when they were pushed to the brink of elimination after Game 4. But the Dodgers have forced this NLCS to the limit.

Corey Seager homered (again). Walker Buehler behaved like a big-game pitcher (again). Mookie Betts made the play of the day (yes, again) and the Dodgers white-knuckled their way through the final three innings to beat the Atlanta Braves, 3-1, in Game 6 on Saturday.

"We did what we had to do to force a Game 7," Dodgers third baseman Justin Turner said.

"But we're not done. We still have a lot to accomplish. We've got a big one tomorrow. We've got to get prepared, come in and fight for every pitch and find a way to win a ballgame."

Put aside your fantasy football team for a day. By winning back-to-back games after falling behind 3-1 in the best-of-seven series the Dodgers have flipped the odds to their favor for Game 7.

When an LCS (American or National League) featuring a 3-1 lead is pushed to a Game 7, the team that faced a 3-1 deficit has won Game 7 in seven of nine instances (before Saturday's ALCS Game 7).

The Dodgers' hitters — particularly their lefties — were tamed by Max Fried's ability to throw his breaking pitches for strikes in Game 1. Fifty of his 96 pitches in six innings that night were either curveballs or sliders. Thirty-two of them were strikes. The Dodgers swung at 18 of them, missed eight. Seven of those swings and misses were by Seager, Max Muncy or Cody Bellinger.

This time around, Fried's first five breaking balls were fouled off, hammered for a 413-foot home run by Seager (his third in four at-bats), taken twice by Muncy as he worked a walk (for the seventh consecutive postseason game) and ripped into right field for an RBI single by Bellinger.

"He kept us off-balance with that all night the last time we faced him. So we figured we'd see it early and we'd try to attack it," Seager said.

"We weren't really sure Game 1. You hadn't faced the guy. You don't really have that much knowledge. You kind of watch him throwing against other teams but we're kind of different. Guys normally pitch us differently. It's a battle that first game to kind of see it out, feel it out."

Seager's homer was his fifth in this NLCS (tying the record for any postseason history while setting the NLCS and franchise records) and sixth of the postseason (a Dodgers record). His 11 RBIs in the NLCS and 15 in the postseason are NLCS and franchise records, respectively.

Turner followed Seager's latest longball with one of his own (on a sinker) and the Dodgers were off to a 3-0 head start following the first inning.

Corey Seager homered in the top of the first inning for the first run of Game 6. (AP Images)

Fried was elusive the rest of the day. The Dodgers had eight hits and drew four walks in his 6-2/3 innings, but only one Dodgers runner advanced past first base after Bellinger's RBI single. Ground balls by Seager and Turner in the fourth couldn't make anything of that.

Meanwhile, Buehler and Betts were extending themselves to keep the Braves off the scoreboard.

As a rookie in 2018, the Dodgers gave Buehler the ball in Game 3 of their Division Series against the Braves, looking to close the series out in Atlanta.

In the bottom of the second, though, the Braves loaded the bases against Buehler who fell behind 3-and-1 to Ronald Acuña Jr.

Acuña crushed a grand slam and the Dodgers went on to lose that game, 6-5, closing the series out at home instead.

Nine postseason starts farther into his evolution as a big-game pitcher, Buehler looks back at that an important part of his education.

"I've failed in those moments. I can handle that failure," he said Saturday. "I've been through it and I've been good after it. That failure doesn't really scare me anymore. Obviously, you don't want to fail. But there's a different feeling when you're not scared of that failure.

"I don't think you think about it. But I think it obviously plays a role. … Those failures teach you things."

He was faced with a similar situation Saturday at Globe Life Field.

The Dodgers had just given him a lead, but the Braves led off the top of the second with three consecutive singles, loading the bases with no outs. A wizened Buehler responded with 10 consecutive pitches thrown at 98 mph or higher. He struck out Austin Riley on three pitches (98, 98 and 99), made veteran Nick Markakis look helpless on a called third strike (99.7 mph) then got Cristian Pache to bounce an 0-and-2 slider to Seager.

"(Catcher Austin) Barnes steered me through it and that's all there really is to it," Buehler said. "The way he was able to guide me through that inning was as good as I've ever seen.

"You have all these game plans and things that you want to do or want to try and do. At the end of the day, I think Barnes has the best view of the baseball and what it's doing out of my hand of anyone on the baseball field. Him and Will (Smith), I'm going to trust what they see and what they want to do more than my guess."

That might have been the highlight of the day for the Dodgers. But Betts stole the show.

With two outs and a runner on first in the fifth, Marcell Ozuna drove a fly ball 378 feet to right field. Betts met it at the wall, leaping up and catching it at the height of his jump.

He landed as a 5-foot-9 bundle of adrenaline. The veins on his neck stood out as he screamed repeatedly "Let's goooo!" — with an adjective occasionally tossed in — high-stepping back to the dugout.

"That's an unbelievable play by an unbelievable player at a big moment," Seager said. "That's what you need at this time of year."

Buehler got through six innings, the third time in his postseason career he has thrown at least six scoreless innings in a start (matching Clayton Kershaw for the most in Dodgers history), and the counting of outs began.

Blake Treinen gave up a run in the seventh while getting his three. Pedro Baez retired the side in the eighth and Kenley Jansen reclaimed the ninth inning for the second consecutive game, retiring the side for his 18th postseason save. ∎

Walker Buehler delivered six scoreless innings for the Dodgers in Game 6, striking out six. (AP Images)

National League Championship Series Game 7

October 18, 2020 • Arlington, Texas
Dodgers 4, Braves 3

'This is Our Year'

HRs from Kiké Hernandez, Cody Bellinger Send Dodgers to World Series

By Bill Plunkett

Like a medieval knight guarding a bridge over a tiny stream, the Dodgers refused to accept the reality of their setbacks.

Lose the first two games of the National League Championship Series? 'Tis but a scratch. Fall behind 3-1 in the series? A mere flesh wound. Spot the Atlanta Braves a 2-0 lead two innings into Game 7? They've had worse.

Unlike the Black Knight of "Holy Grail" lore, though, the Dodgers have lived to fight another day, rallying on home runs by Kiké Hernandez and Cody Bellinger to beat the Braves, 4-3, in an epic tale of a Game 7 on Sunday night at Globe Life Field.

Wounded but not even dead, the Dodgers became the first National League team to fall behind 2-0 and 3-1 in a best-of-seven series and come back to win. (Four American League teams have done it.)

"From the moment that we were able to put a season together — once they figured out the COVID thing — everybody was expecting us to get to the World Series. We were expecting us to get to the World Series," Hernandez said. "Up to the point where we went down 3-1 in this series, we hadn't really gone through any adversity this season. That was the one thing. It was time to get it done.

"It was the first time not just going through adversity but kind of feeling like you've got nothing to lose. They were the ones who had something to lose. You have a 3-1 lead. You shouldn't lose this series. We were able to take it one game at a time, one inning at a time. We were able to pull it off."

The emotion of the moment got to Manager Dave Roberts and he yelled to the limited number of fans in the stands as he accepted the NL championship trophy, "This year is our year. This is our year."

It is the third time in the past four years that the Dodgers will be one of the last two teams standing.

"You know, we've worked our ass off all year," NLCS MVP Corey Seager said. "Following protocols, being away from family at times, being here in the bubble quarantine. It hasn't been easy. We've been up to the challenge and we're sticking with it and we're gonna keep going."

In a matchup of evenly-equipped teams, the Dodgers held one distinct advantage over the Braves — starting pitching. While the Braves have managed with two, maybe three, the Dodgers had five.

Clayton Kershaw's back spasms reworked the equation some, but the Dodgers changed the math entirely, opting to use Dustin May out of the bullpen early in the series, starting him on three days' rest in Game 5 — then bringing him back again after one day off to serve as the "opener" in Game 7.

Roberts explained the decision as a way to give May "the certainty" of when he would pitch and which batters he would face. This "certainty" didn't come until Sunday afternoon, however, and May looked decidedly uncertain as he missed the strike zone with his first eight pitches. Marcell Ozuna cashed in the door prize with an RBI single.

Tony Gonsolin would have been the easy choice to start Game 7. He started Game 2 and was on normal rest. Instead, the Dodgers wanted him to avoid the top of the

Kiké Hernandez celebrates after hitting a home run in the sixth inning to tie Game 7, 3-3. (AP Images)

Dodgers manager Dave Roberts (left) and President of Baseball Operations Andrew Friedman celebrate with the trophy after the Dodgers' thrilling win over the Braves in Game 7 of the NLCS. (AP Images)

THE LOS ANGELES DODGERS' UNFORGETTABLE 2020 WORLD SERIES SEASON

Braves' lineup (Ronald Acuña Jr., Freddie Freeman and Ozuna) until he had settled in.

Robbed of "the certainty" the Dodgers gave May, Gonsolin served up a solo home run to the first batter he faced, Dansby Swanson and — shades of May — back-to-back walks to start the fourth after Will Smith's two-out, two-run single had tied the score in the third.

The Braves regained the lead on an RBI single by Austin Riley and were poised to do so much more when the Dodgers' first hero stepped up.

A wild pitch put runners at second and third with no outs. The Dodgers played their infield at normal depth but when Nick Markakis bounced a ground ball to third baseman Justin Turner he quickly threw home and Swanson was caught in a rundown. Turner ended it with a full-out dive, swiping a tag (barely) on Swanson's leg then popping up and throwing to third base where Seager was covering and Riley had run into a double play, waiting too long to try and replace Markakis at third.

"That was huge. That was huge," Mookie Betts said. "I didn't even see the backside play. I didn't. Once he dove and made the tag I thought the play was over. They were still in pretty decent shape with guys on first and second at that time, with one out.

"That's a big momentum shift."

It was a whole lot of bacon to save on one play and Betts added to the platter an inning later.

For the third consecutive game, the right fielder showed why his glove is golden. With one out in the fifth, Freeman drove him back to the wall. Betts went up — as he did in Game 6 — and came down with the ball, this time having robbed a home run.

"JT's play was huge. Being second and third, no outs and getting out of the inning with only giving up one run," Seager said. "Then Mookie taking away a potential homer — another spark."

That was the Braves' last scoring opportunity. They didn't have another hit and only one baserunner after Turner's play. Whatever they got wrong in their pitching script, they got one thing very right — Julio Urias was brilliant. Handed the ball to start the seventh, Roberts rode him to the end and Urias retired the final nine Braves in order.

"I didn't know Julio was going back out there for the ninth but after I saw him, I was pumped up," Turner said. "He doesn't scare off. He loves to pitch on the big stage, and he's done it all postseason for us."

Urias inherited a tie game when Hernandez came off the bench to face lefty A.J. Minter (the Game 5 starter who shut them out for three innings, striking out seven of 10 Dodgers he faced) in the sixth.

Before Game 6, Hernandez described the pre-game clubhouse activities as "some screaming, a little bit of dancing — mostly by me."

There was more of the same when he ended an eight-pitch at-bat against Minter by turning on a fastball and sending it into the left field seats to tie the score.

An inning later, the same buildup ended with the same result, Bellinger taking Chris Martin eight pitches into the at-bat before launching the go-ahead home run into the right field seats. It was the Dodgers' first lead of the deciding game.

"Two strikes, I was in battle mode. It was one of those where as soon as I hit it, I knew I got it," Bellinger said.

For all the disappointment of the follow-up to his MVP season and his often poor performance at the plate in the postseason, the home run was Bellinger's 22nd in the seventh inning or later since the start of 2019 (regular season and postseason), the most in the majors.

"We took care of business against the Brewers. We took care of business against the Padres. And we took care of business against the Braves," Hernandez said. "It was a little harder than we thought it would be. But I'm glad we pulled it off." ∎

SOUTHERN CALIFORNIA
NEWS GROUP

Los Angeles Daily News
dailynews.com

THE ORANGE COUNTY
REGISTER
ocregister.com

PRESS-TELEGRAM
presstelegram.com

DAILY BREEZE
dailybreeze.com

THE PRESS-ENTERPRISE
pe.com

Pasadena Star-News
pasadenastarnews.com

**INLAND VALLEY
DAILY BULLETIN**
dailybulletin.com

THE SUN
sbsun.com

Redlands Daily Facts
redlandsdailyfacts.com

SAN GABRIEL VALLEY TRIBUNE
sgvtribune.com

Whittier Daily News
whittierdailynews.com

digitalfirst
M E D I A

Local Brand Leaders — Known and Trusted for Over 100 Years

As premium local content providers, each of the SCNG newspapers has a long history of editorial excellence in their own respective markets — forming a special kind of trust and brand loyalty that readers really value. Exclusive local content sets the Southern California News Group apart, providing readers and users with news and information they won't find anywhere else. From local elections to their home team's top scores, when area residents need late-breaking news, SCNG newspapers, websites and mobile media are their number one resource.